Cheatin' Hearts

by

Paul Ledoux
and
David Smyth

Playwrights Canada Press
Toronto • Canada

Cheatin' Hearts © Copyright 1995 Paul Ledoux & David Smyth
Playwrights Canada Press is the publishing imprint of
the Playwrights Union of Canada (PUC): 54 Wolseley St., 2nd fl.
Toronto, Ontario CANADA M5T 1A5
Tel: (416) 703-0201 Fax: (416) 703-0059

Playwrights Canada Press operates with the generous assistance
of The Canada Council - Writing and Publishing Section, and Theatre
Section, the Ontario Arts Council, and the Ontario Publishing Centre.

Cover: Set drawing by Ted Rogers. Photo of Jen Foster by: Helen Tansey.
Cover design by Paul Ledoux and Tony Hamill.
Playwrights' photo by Bruce Nickson.

Canadian Cataloguing in Publication Data
Paul Ledoux, 1949 —
        Cheatin' hearts
A play
ISBN 0-88754-536-X
I. Smyth, David, 1948—   II. Title.
PS8573.E3439C5   1995   C812'.54   C95-931238-2
PR9199.3.L43C5   1995

First edition: May 1995.
Printed and bound in Winnipeg, Manitoba, Canada.

Cheatin' Hearts

Cheatin' Hearts is dedicated,
with love, to Ferne Downey and Rachel Smyth

Paul Ledoux, (l) and David Smyth

Paul Ledoux was born in Halifax, Nova Scotia. His first play, *The Electrical Man*, won the Quebec Drama Festival Award for Best Play (1976). Since that time, he has had 26 plays produced, including *The Secret Garden*, adapted from the novel by Francis Hodgson Burnett (published in *Class Acts* by Playwrights Canada Press), *Honky Tonk Angels* with Ferne Downey, and two colloborations with David Young: *Love Is Strange* (published in *The CTR Anthology*), and the Dora Mavor Moore and Chalmers Award winning *Fire* (Blizzard Publishing). Electronic media credits include: *Street Legal*, *The Campbells*, and CBC Radio's popular *Booster McCrane PM*.

David Smyth is a guitartist, musical director, composer, and playwright. He began his career in Thunder Bay playing with local bands with long-time friend, Paul Shaffer. In the Sixties, he moved to Toronto, joining seminal Canadian blues band, *Whisky Howl*. His career in theatre began as a member of the pit band for the legendary Toronto production of *Godspell* which featured future "Second City" luminaries Gilda Radner, Martin Short, and John Candy. In 1993, he appeared in the CBC-televised cast reunion special, "Friends of Gilda".

Smyth was the musical director on the original Magnus Theatre production of *Fire* and the subsequent national tour. He went on to collaborate with Ledoux on music for *As Time Goes By*, and finally to create *Cheatin' Hearts*.

Work as a musical director also includes *18Wheels, Rock and Roll, Just a Closer Walk with Patsy Cline*, and *Cheatin' Hearts*. As a guitarist, he accompanied performers as diverse as Bob Hope, Koko Taylor, Gene Pitney, Colleen Peterson, The Mamas and the Papas, and Bo Diddlely.

Foreword

Oh, the bars...no matter how much success a career in music might bring, if a long period of dues-paying has been spent in the bars, they loom over your shoulder — an ever-present spectre reminding you where you came from, hinting at calling you back.

The oily hustlers, amateur contests, stolen songs, the incestuous social scene, the promises, the lies, the hope, the beer — it's all in here.

And wherever there is music, and wherever there are dreams, here it will always be.

Joan Besen
Prairie Oyster
March, 1995

Playwright's Notes

It would be impossible to deny that we've spent a goodly portion of the last twenty-five years of our lives hanging out in bars. From very early on, the opportunity to hear and play live music lead us to the "low-tone hi-spots" that were the inspiration for *Cheatin' Hearts*. The play itself grew out of a long series of tall tales exchanged between the two of us as we struggled to find the core of our story. Be it our home towns of Thunder Bay, Halifax, or anywhere else you can think of in this country, you'll find the characters who inhabit *Cheatin' Hearts* playing in taverns, Legion Halls, and honky tonks.

While *Cheatin' Hearts* is a work of fiction, there's nothing in it that hasn't happened to someone we've met or heard about in honky tonks, spanning this country, as surly as those rusty old CNR tracks. So, although this published version of *Cheatin' Hearts* is set in Thunder Bay, in every production to date we've changed the script to accommodate local references. We would encourage you to imagine the setting is your home town and local references to people, places and things are as familiar to you as the bar in the Adanac Hotel is to David, or Open Mike at Ginger's Tavern is to me.

Paul Ledoux
May 2, 1995

The authors would like to thank the following groups and individuals whose support made *Cheatin' Hearts* possible:

Mario Crudo
Iris Turcotte
The Arts Club Theatre
Michael Ardenne
Bob Balabuk
Babbs Chula
Diane De Greuters
Jenny Dean
Ferne Downey
Danny Johnson
David McLeod
Cathy Nosaty
Dennis O'Conor
Colleen Peterson
Haley Tyson
David Weir

Michael McLaughlin
Canadian Stage Company
Bill Millard
Joan Besen
Danny Cash
Jenny Clarke
Melanie Doane
Ross Douglas
Lee Johnson
Pete Klippensoein
Mary Ann MacDonald
Ontario Arts Council
Donna O'Connor
Richard Smyth
Lori Valleau
Lenore Zann

Production History

Cheatin' Hearts premiered at Magnus Theatre, Thunder Bay, Ontario, March 24, 1994, with the following cast and crew:

DANIELLE	*Paula Boudreau*
DRUMMER	*Wayne Breiland*
LINDA	*Jennifer Foster*
HOSS	*Terry V. Hart*
STAN	*Danny Johnson*
BOBBY	*Kim Kondrashoff*
BASS PLAYER	*John Myers*
KELLY	*Colette Wise*

Directed by Mario Crudo.
Musical director - David Smyth.
Set and lighting design by Ted Roberts.
Costume design by Riitta Hirvasova
Stage manager - Merrilee Houston.

Cheatin' Hearts was subsequently produced by Globe Theatre, Regina, Saskatchewan, October, 1994, with the following cast and crew:

STAN	*Tom Arntzen*
DANIELLE	*Paula Boudreau*
KELLY	*Beverley Elliott*
GUITARIST	*Dennis Ficor*
LINDA	*Jennifer Foster*
DRUMMER	*Paul Kenny*
BOBBY	*Andy Maton*
BASS GUITAR	*Brett Schinbein*
HOSS	*Allan Zinyk*

Directed by Robert McQueen.
Musical director - David Smyth.
Set and costume design by Pearl Bellesen.
Lighting design by James Milburn.
Stage manager - Teresa Hiorns.
Assistant stage manager - Dani Phillipson.
Apprentice stage manager - Michael Bigayan.

Act One, Scene One

*The Golden Horseshoe is a garish country bar.
Barn board predominates. Saddles, old tack and
neon beer signs decorate the room. Off to one
side there's a stage littered with gear. In front of
the stage there's a small dance floor, beyond that
a few tables. Along the far wall there's a place to
sit at stools, and put your drink on a "bar"
attached to the wall. There's a pay phone near the
downstage entrance. Upstage, partially obscured,
is the wet bar where drinks may be ordered but
the bartender need not be seen. There may also be
a fire exit in this area and a set of stairs leading
up to the "dressing room".*

*The dressing room is, in reality, a storeroom.
Cases of beer line the walls but there's a rack for
clothes, a bar table and a dressing table with a
mirror. There is also an exit to the staff
washroom.*

*At rise the dressing room is not visible. Lights
up on the bar. HOSS, a big guy in a garish
cowboy shirt and white Stetson, enters carrying
an empty two-four of beer. He puts it on the bar
and collects empties. STAN, a slightly foggy
looking guy in a baggy gray suit sits at a table
with a big glass of scotch before him.*

HOSS   Howdy. Ain't seen you 'round here before. My name is Hoss.

> *HOSS offers his hand. STAN looks up, a little confused.*

STAN   What? Like *Bonanza*?

HOSS   Yeah, *Bonanza*.

STAN   Ah...wild...Stan.

> *STAN shakes HOSS' hand.*

HOSS   Hi Wild Stan. Hoss. I am a country/western singer. It's true. I sing Jimmy Rodgers and Hank and Elvis the King. It's great. I sing and all the people clap me. Say; "Sing more Hoss".

STAN   So, you're a star.

HOSS   You bet I are. *(laughs)* In this here bar. *(laughs harder)* Yeah! Night times when all the neon beer signs is turned on flashin' blue and red like now and people get in line doin' "Ackey Breaky" and all that? Sweat coming down off everybody, I think I died and gone to heaven.

> *A pause. STAN isn't impressed by HOSS' revelations.*

HOSS   I clean up too!

STAN   Yeah?

HOSS   Yeah. Know how I got my job?

STAN   No man, how'd you get your job?

HOSS   I won a talent contest!

> *STAN looks at him like HOSS is out of his mind.*

HOSS   It's true. See, Thursday night is Open Mike. Anybody can get up and sing and maybe win a prize. So one time — I do it! I sing "Teddy Bear".

> *HOSS does a very clumsy imitation of Elvis' signature moves.*

Mister Man! Everybody laughs then smashes their hands together! What a good feeling! And I win a gift certificate for "Arby's" Stack-o-beef and Coke too! And Bobby, he owns the band, he tells me; "Come back." And I do! He gets me this job I come back so much.

STAN   Bobby "owns" the band?

HOSS   Sure. He's "the man", Stan.

STAN   You mean he's the boss, Hoss.

HOSS   (*laughs*) Yeah, and he's my best friend too.

STAN   No kiddin'.

HOSS   Surprised aren't ya? He is a big star, but he's not snotty. We can always make each other laugh.

STAN   Yeah? We talking *Hee Haw*, or what?

HOSS   Nah, witty banter — that's our style. Bobby says I'm the kind of guy makes everybody forget their troubles. I am proud to do that.

> *STAN takes a big haul on his scotch as BOBBY, a cool looking dude in a silk jacket, comes out of the washroom, straightening his cowboy hat.*

HOSS   There's Bobby now. Bobby! Bobby!

BOBBY sees them and walks over.

HOSS   Bobby, my man, this is Wild Stan.

BOBBY   You're late.

STAN   Sorry I...

BOBBY   Forget the excuse. I've heard 'em all.

STAN   Perfect. You didn't tell me it's Open Mike...

BOBBY   It's part of the job and if you can handle it you can handle the job. Follow?

STAN   I can follow anything, just don't expect me to look jubilant.

BOBBY   Don't worry, that's my job, and after three years in this dump I can smile with my hat on fire.

HOSS   Come on Bobby. Get happy. It's Talent Night.

BOBBY   Hoss, they're using Bobby Curtis T-shirts to wipe down the bar, the sound guy's stoned again and this afternoon I saw the owner talking to a karaoke salesman. What have I got to be happy about?

HOSS   Look around ya! Everybody's here.

BOBBY   Yeah. The guy with the tuba showed up.

HOSS   Yeah, and he said he'd never come back after you poured that beer down his horn!

BOBBY   And the Turbo Twins are here...again.

HOSS   Yeah and they got that new colour of hair too. Things is some hot tonight!

BOBBY   Hoss, the musical highlight of the evening came in the last set — and it was Peg-Leg Palusso's singing "Phantom 309".

HOSS   A classic!

BOBBY   Remember that table dancer I was seeing?

HOSS   (*thinks about it*) Bubbles?

BOBBY   That very unhappy biker in the corner is her ex-husband.

HOSS   Probably just wants to say "Thanks".

> *BOBBY cracks up and pats HOSS on the back.*

BOBBY   (*to STAN*) Time to start the second set.

> *BOBBY gets on stage and the other musicians follow.*

STAN   Now there's a man at peace with himself.

> *STAN stands up.*

HOSS   Oh Bobby gets blue sometimes but he's way better than them karaokes. Everybody loves him. Why, he could be house band here for life.

STAN   Another vision of hell. Excuse me. Show time.

> *STAN starts to cross towards the bandstand as the band members get set. HOSS follows STAN.*

HOSS   You gonna play?

STAN   What choice do I have? My rent's over-due.

HOSS   But you can't win rent, just like...prizes.

STAN   Hoss I'm not here for the competition. I came here to
                do an audition.

                *HOSS looks amazed and then laughs as STAN
                sits at the piano and plays a flashy arpeggio.*

BOBBY   We're back. All right. Hey it's Thursday night!
                Anybody know what that means?

HOSS   Talent night!

BOBBY   That's right, Talent Night! Every Thursday night we
                give all you fabulous performers out there the chance
                to play with a truly tight band. (*as the band does a
                sloppy shot, BOBBY winces.*) Sort of a country
                karaoke thang — and we have some great prizes for
                tonight's best act. SO...one, two, three, four...

                *The band hits it hard, playing a rocker. BOBBY
                sings and works the audience like the old pro that
                he is.*

CADILLAC CAR

BOBBY   The first one that I owned it was a '48 hearse
                Man it was the greatest, Daddy said it was the worst
                The rollers in the back were great for loading gear
                Drummer said; "It's haunted".
                I said; "Have another beer".

                Six chicks in the back seat, music cranked up loud
                Talk about prestige, make a young man proud
                We went headin' down the highway, feelin' super fine
                I rolled her in Blind River, hitchhiked home in '69.

                But so what? It was a Cadillac car .
                Guess I showed them all that I was a star
                I was travelin' fast, travelin' far
                Some day I'll drive a brand new Cadillac car.

                I got a '53 ragtop when that first hit came around
                She cost six hundred dollars, so I put fifty down
                On that V8 El Dorado candy-apple red
                A back seat bigger than a king-size double bed

Leather seats, power steering
I put steer horns on the hood
Man I showed those mothers
I could treat their daughters good
It was 1987 when that heap got finally sold
It had holes in the top and the winters here get cold.

But so what? It was a Cadillac car
Guess I showed them all that I was a star
I was travelin' fast, travelin' far
Some day I'll drive a brand new Cadillac car.

I bought a '68 Fleetwood with a big 3-7-5
Vinyl seats, "real plush", power windows, power glide
When I drove up to the Legion
Ladies still gave me the eye
I was selling records from the trunk
Guess some dreams never die

Playin' round the honky tonks
Might bring a small man down
But listen to this baby we're the best band in this town
I'm a big star in this bar. My act still has some class
But I don't drive my Caddie 'cause I can't afford the gas.

But so what? It was a Cadillac car
Guess I showed them all that I was a star
I was travelin' fast, travelin' far
Some day I'll drive a brand new Cadillac car.
Some day I'll drive a brand new Cadillac car.
Some day I'll drive a brand new Cadillac car.

As BOBBY sings, three women enter; LINDA
MCGEE, shy, gawky, in her early twenties,
dressed in a baggy sweater and faded jeans. She
carries a guitar case and looks scared to death as
she hovers near the entrance. Then she's pushed
towards the empty table by DANIELLE
DUCHARME, who is in her early thirties, sexy,
dressed in a red leather mini-skirt, a silver
spangled cowboy shirt, matching embroidered
bolero jacket and high-heeled cowboy boots that
match the outfit. Obviously this is a woman
who watches The Nashville Network with some
care. She eyes BOBBY, then STAN as he takes a
break. She dances, attracting both BOBBY and
STAN's attention. KELLY CONNERS follows.
Late thirties, wearing a studded jeans jacket that's

a few years out of style and a bit tight. Her hair is in an untrimmed shag. She eyes the band with a certain hard-bitten cynicism.

BOBBY sees her and grins. He points at her and winks. KELLY nods, then sits down, hauls out a pack of Players and lights up. DANIELLE heads for the bar while LINDA fumbles with her guitar case, sliding it under a table.

DANIELLE orders at the bar, then hauls out a cigarette case — a Balkan Sobranie with its distinctive black paper and gold tip. She lights the smoke, watching BOBBY intently while waiting for her order. As the song ends she returns to the table with two mugs full of shooters. HOSS leads the applause for the band and cheers. BOBBY takes a bow.

BOBBY   OK, we're gonna take a pause for "The Cause" and be right back.

The band plays "Bobby's Bump", their signature tag, as BOBBY hops off the stage and approaches the table. HOSS, intrigued by BOBBY's strange behaviour, grabs a beer case and starts picking up bottles, working his way over to the table.

BOBBY   Kelly?

KELLY   Hello, Robert.

BOBBY hooks a chair and sits down.

BOBBY   I don't believe it. How long you been a redhead?

KELLY   Let's see...I dumped purple in '92...

BOBBY laughs.

BOBBY	Right...you were doing that thing with the Metal band...
KELLY	"Tube Steak".
BOBBY	Yeah, "Tube Steak". They had that bald drummer with the tattoo on his head. What was his name?
KELLY	Brain Damage.
BOBBY	Right. Twisted...whooo! What ever happened to him?
KELLY	I married him.
BOBBY	You and Brain Damage?
	BOBBY whistles softly.
KELLY	The divorce went through about a year ago.
BOBBY	Oh, sorry.
KELLY	You kiddin'? Ever try living with someone who's about to implode?
	BOBBY laughs. DANIELLE, trying to get attention, laughs a bit too loudly. BOBBY glances at her.
DANIELLE	Hi! I'm Danielle.
KELLY	Oh! Sorry.
DANIELLE	(*to KELLY*) Of course you are. (*to BOBBY*) And this is Linda.
BOBBY	Hi. Bobby.
LINDA	Hi Bobby.

DANIELLE hands him a shooter. He takes the evil looking drink and holds it up.

BOBBY What's this?

DANIELLE A "Screw Me To The Wall".

BOBBY My favourite.

BOBBY toasts DANIELLE. They clink test tubes and drink. HOSS scoops up the empties.

DANIELLE So, Kelly said you two used to play together.

KELLY Back when I was a child star.

BOBBY laughs and looks back at KELLY.

BOBBY The T-Bay Tanya Tucker.

HOSS Geeze are you Kelly? Wow. Wow, Bobby, it's Kelly! Bobby told me about you all the time.

They all look up at HOSS.

BOBBY Ah...Hoss Cartright. My protégé.

HOSS shakes hands with everybody.

KELLY Hi.

HOSS Hi. Hoss. (*to DANIELLE*) Hi. Hoss.

DANIELLE Hi, Hoss.

HOSS (*to LINDA*) Hi Hoss.

LINDA Pleased to meet you, Hoss.

HOSS Thanks. You're Kelly's friend, eh?

LINDA	That's right.
HOSS	Her and Bobby had a big hit record you know. "Back in the dark ages", right Bobby?
BOBBY	That's right Hoss. Listen, why don't you get the ladies another round.
HOSS	No fuss and no fight!

HOSS hurries off to get the drinks.

BOBBY	(*to KELLY*) So, when'd you get back?
KELLY	'Bout a year and a half ago.
BOBBY	And you never looked me up?
KELLY	I swore I'd never speak to you again. Remember?
BOBBY	Ah...yeah.

BOBBY laughs nervously, then looks down at LINDA's guitar case.

BOBBY	So you gonna get up?
DANIELLE	You bet we are. We've got a great song that Linda wrote.
LINDA	Ah, I don't know.
KELLY	Maybe.
BOBBY	What's the problem?
KELLY	See the guy with the tuba?
BOBBY	He just sits there. Honest, he never gets up.

KELLY   Right. He just sits there.

BOBBY   And plays along. Starting about half-way through his
               next draft. (*smiles broadly*). So, whenever you're
               ready...

               BOBBY stands and heads for the stage.

DANIELLE   OK, let's go.

LINDA   (*nervous*) We should just come back some other
               night.

DANIELLE   Some other night!

LINDA   Sure, like, maybe five years from now.

DANIELLE   Linda, we are not doing *your* song in Kelly's kitchen
               for another five minutes, never mind five years and
               we are sure as hell not waiting for that guy to have
               another beer.

LINDA   I can't. I can't do it. The song sucks and we're going
               to fall flat on our face.

DANIELLE   Kelly?

KELLY   Reality check. Danielle?

DANIELLE   It's nine-thirty on Thursday night in Fort William.

KELLY   And if we screw up, they ain't gonna talk about it on
               TNN.

               HOSS brings over another round of shooters.

BOBBY	(*on mike*) OK folks, we've got three lovely young ladies who really want to come up here and sing, but they're shy — so let's give them a little encouragement. Danielle, Linda, and Kelly , (*like on "Let's Make A Deal"*) Come on down!
LINDA	Oh God.

> *DANIELLE hauls some "charts" out of her purse. KELLY hands out shooters. They toast.*

DANIELLE	(*sings*) Ahhhh...
LINDA	(*harmony*) Ahhhh...
KELLY	(*harmony*) Ahhhh...
ALL	(*they scream*) Ah!!!

> *They put their drinks back. LINDA gets her guitar, takes a deep breath and follows KELLY and DANIELLE to the stage.*

BOBBY	(*on mike*) All right! Look at these ladies! Beautiful! So Linda, what are you going to do for us tonight?

> *LINDA tries to speak but stammers instead. DANIELLE jumps in.*

DANIELLE	It's a song Linda wrote, Bobby.
BOBBY	That's great and what's it called, Linda?
DANIELLE	It's called "Nothing Like A Friend", Bobby. Go on Linda.
BOBBY	OK. Here they are...
LINDA	"Daddy's Girls."

KELLY &
DANIELLE (*a new name they hate*) "Daddy's Girls"?

DANIELLE hands out the song charts.

DANIELLE Here you are.

The Bass player and Drummer look at the charts in horror — neither of them read music. STAN however grabs his chart and scans it avidly.

BOBBY Just follow the ladies boys. "Daddy's Girls" singing "Friends"!!!

LINDA starts woodenly playing the changes on the guitar, the bass hits a couple of wrong notes. DANIELLE looks terrified and leans towards STAN.

DANIELLE Help!

STAN gives DANIELLE a big intro which ignites the band. She beams at him, takes the gum out of her mouth, sticks it to the mike stand and starts to sing lead. HOSS stands to one side — falling in love— with LINDA.

(THERE AIN'T) NOTHING LIKE A FRIEND

DANIELLE Yeah we're fightin, the way we always do
And he's been drinking, so tonight I'm callin' you
Sometimes you need somebody
Who can help your heart to mend.
When you're hurtin' there ain't nothing like a friend

You are his best friend,
And you know I love him too
But sometimes baby, love can't pull you through
And you know I get so restless
Think there's just no hope in sight
Then I need you just like I need you tonight.

A friend will never tell you lies
A friend will never say good-bye
He'll give you shelter
When you need someplace to hide
He'll defend you to the end
On you I can depend
A friend will always stay, right by your side.

And tomorrow is just another day
Same as always I'll be on my way
And I'll say; "I owe you honey"
As I slip out your back door
And then you'll smile and say;
"Baby, that's what friends are for."

The song ends. HOSS leads the applause.

BOBBY   All right! "Daddy's Girls."

They bow clumsily and get off the stage. HOSS keeps cheering

BOBBY   OK, next up we got a real pro. Hoss! Get your happy ass up here!

The band goes into a vamp and HOSS, grinning from ear to ear, starts towards the stage. As he's passing LINDA he stops, inspired.

HOSS   You play real good, Linda.

LINDA   Thanks!

HOSS   Come sing with me OK? I'm doin' "Everybody's Favourite Singing Cowboy".

LINDA   "Everybody's Favourite Singing Cowboy"!

HOSS   It's a real good one.

LINDA   (*smiles*) It sure is.

HOSS   OK then — come on!

HOSS grabs her hand and drags her back on stage.

BOBBY   OK. Here he is folks — everybody's favourite singing cowboy, the inimitable Hoss Cartright.

HOSS gets on stage and tips his hat to the crowd.

HOSS   Hi Hoss. And...and this is Linda back to help. Thanks. Here's my song. You sing too, OK?

HOSS sings. LINDA looks a bit confused during the first verse but joins in on the chorus adding flourishes like she's been singing the following song her whole life.

EVERYBODY'S FAVOURITE SINGING COWBOY

HOSS   When I walk in through the door
Everybody shakes my hand
I tip my hat to the ladies and I sit in with the band
They say; "Howdy Hoss

BOBBY   Howdy Hoss!

HOSS   Why don't you sing a cowboy song
Sing "King Of The Road" and we'll all play along"
Sing about ol' Shep and what a friend a dog can be
I'm a star in this country bar
And all I do is "Act Naturally"

LINDA joins in.

BOTH   'Cause I'm everybody's favourite singing cowboy
And that's all that I ever want to be
There's something special happens
Every time I sing a song
Everybody shouts and cheers and claps for me

HOSS   Oh I'm a local hero everybody knows my name

BOBBY   Hoss!

HOSS   Sit right back and have a beer
              I'll make you glad you came
              I'll sing some old Gene Autry tunes
              Hank Snow and Frankie Lane
              And then do good old "Bud The Spud"
              That's how I earned my fame

LINDA   Oh some folks get so lonely
              Living on their own
              Some folks never find a friend
              Some folks got no home
              But when I'm up here singing
              I never can feel sad
              Looking at those laughin' faces
              Always makes me glad.

                   HOSS is amazed LINDA not only knows his
                   song, but sings like she's been doing it her
                   whole life.

BOTH   (That) I'm everybody's favourite singing cowboy
              And that's all that I ever want to be
              There's something special happens
              Every time I sing a song
              Everybody shouts and cheers and claps for me
              I'm everybody's favourite singing cowboy.
              I'm everybody's favourite singing cowboy.
              I'm everybody's favourite singing cowboy.

BOBBY   Everybody's favourite singing cowboy! Hoss
              Cartright! Anybody else want to sing? Good. I'll be
              right back with the winners real soon. And remember
              it's still 'Buy the Band a Beer Week.' So...

BAND   Buy us a beer!

                   Band plays "Singing Cowboy" as a tag. HOSS
                   follows LINDA as she gets off stage. BOBBY is
                   right behind them. STAN immediately heads for
                   the bar where DANIELLE is ordering, keeping
                   her eye on BOBBY and LINDA. She absent-
                   mindedly fishes out a cigarette. STAN, not
                   missing a beat, lights it. She smiles at him.

HOSS	Thank you. (*off mike*) Geeze, Linda. You knew my song.
LINDA	(*smiles*) I haven't heard it in years!
HOSS	That's 'cause Bobby and me just wrote it.

LINDA is flabbergasted.

LINDA	You and Bobby wrote that song?
HOSS	Yeah, well, I brung him some words and that and he...
BOBBY	Good stuff, Linda.

LINDA glares at BOBBY.

LINDA	That's a Tex McGee song!
HOSS	No. I wrote words and Bobby...
BOBBY	Tex McGee...
LINDA	My father.

LINDA walks away. BOBBY goes after her.

BOBBY	Linda...listen...
LINDA	You ripped off my father.
BOBBY	I know. I know. I'm sorry.

HOSS hovers near them looking very concerned. BOBBY glances at him.

HOSS	Everything OK, Bobby?
BOBBY	Sure, sure. Beverages? Beer. Get one for Linda too.

HOSS	No fuss, no fight. I'll get the beer — all right.

HOSS goes for beers.

LINDA I don't want a beer.

BOBBY Just let me explain, OK? Hoss comes in with some words scrawled on a table napkin. He asks me to help him write "his song". I sit down and the tune comes to me and then the chorus and...I knock this thing off for Hoss. I hadn't heard Tex in ten years! Wasn't 'till I heard Hoss sing it that I realized what I'd done. I couldn't tell him "his song" belonged to somebody else. It'd break his heart.

HOSS approaches with the beers.

HOSS Here's the beverages.

LINDA Thanks, Hoss.

HOSS Bobby tell you how we wrote the song?

LINDA Yeah. It just kind of sounded like one of my daddy's.

HOSS Your daddy?

BOBBY Tex McGee. Used to play that tavern in Doubreville.

LINDA The Royalton.

BOBBY Tex was real good. Too good for that dive.

HOSS Must have been 'cause his daughter's so good too. Linda wrote that "Friend" song you know. (*sings*) 'When you're lonesome, there ain't nothing like a friend'. Yeah. It's got to be a good song if I remember it!

DANIELLE and KELLY rejoin the table.

BOBBY   OK, the song gets the nod, how about the singers?

HOSS   (*blushing*) Aw gee, Bobby.

BOBBY   You think they should win, Hoss?

HOSS   'Course they should win.

BOBBY   OK, well let's go find out if they did.

BOBBY stands and heads for the bandstand.
HOSS grins at the girls.

HOSS   Betcha you win.

BOBBY   (*on mike*) OK, the judge's votes are in on tonight's contest and here's Hoss to tell you who the winners are!

HOSS   Geeze Bobby, I don't even know who the judges was.

BOBBY   You was the judges Hoss. Get your happy ass up here.

HOSS beams and leans into the mike.

HOSS   Ah...ah OK...Hi. I'm the judges. Ah, Hoss. There were some real good acts tonight and all that, but...ah...there was this one group that was way the best...The winner is (*drum roll*) Daddy's Girls. Linda, Kelly and...and, uh...

HOSS forgets DANIELLE's name. She waves at the crowd.

DANIELLE Danielle!

HOSS   Danielle!

BOBBY   Let's hear it for them! Daddy's Girls!

> *Applause, led by BOBBY and HOSS. The girls*
> *stand and go to the stage*

BOBBY And tonight's special prizes are courtesy of Esthetics by Cherie of Inter-City Mall. If it's beauty — it's Cherie.

> *BOBBY hauls out three envelopes and hands*
> *them to the girls. DANIELLE leans into the*
> *mike.*

DANIELLE Thank you, Bobby. This is wonderful. Did you know that Cherie offers the widest range of beauty services in Northwestern Ontario?

BOBBY No I didn't. Guess you must be a regular customer.

DANIELLE I'm more than just a customer. I'm the Cherie colour consultant.

> *DANIELLE gives BOBBY a big smooch. They*
> *break off and laugh. BOBBY goes to hug*
> *KELLY, but she slides away and heads back to*
> *her table. The band plays Daddy's Girls off.*
> *BOBBY follows them.*

KELLY Smooth plug for Cherie. The boss will be proud.

DANIELLE I promised to do it. How do you think I got the night off?

> *BOBBY sits down with the girls.*

DANIELLE That was great. Thanks, Bobby.

BOBBY You deserved it.

LINDA You really like our song?

BOBBY It needs work, but it could be a hit.

DANIELLE	(*protective*) "Friends" is fine just like it is!

> *BOBBY sits, all business.*

BOBBY	It needs a hook.
KELLY	"There ain't nothin' like a friend" is a pretty good hook.
BOBBY	Not when it's buried in the verse.
LINDA	God. I'm an idiot.
DANIELLE	We could fix that — easy.
BOBBY	Sure. (*to LINDA*) You written any more material?
DANIELLE	You kiddin'? She spends half her life banging away on that old Gibson.
BOBBY	I'd love to hear some more.
LINDA	Well...sure!
DANIELLE	That could be arranged!

> *DANIELLE leans in trying to be sexy, but topples her drink. BOBBY jumps to avoid it.*

DANIELLE	Oh great. Sorry.
BOBBY	That's cool, you missed.
DANIELLE	No, that is a terrible thing to do...(*shifting gears*) ...to the influential local organizer of "The Cross Canada Country Countdown". You think we're good enough to represent Northern Ontario?
LINDA	Danielle.

BOBBY	Sure, but you'll have to rehearse your butts off to go all the way.
DANIELLE	I agree, but we'll need help. Interested?
LINDA	Oh God...
BOBBY	Maybe. We're rehearsing tomorrow if you want to...
KELLY	Time out. I'm retired. We just came down for some fun, remember?
DANIELLE	Come on Kelly...if Bobby can help us...
KELLY	I'm serious. I got my kid and my job, and rehearsals take too much time...
BOBBY	Whoo. Whoo, back up — kid? You've got a kid? Damn. And "I Knew The Bride When She Used To Rock and Roll".
KELLY	Hey baby — I can still rock and roll.
DANIELLE	Damn right. She's great and she'll do it.
KELLY	That's not what I meant.
DANIELLE	It is definitely what you meant.
BOBBY	Could be a lot of fun, Kelly — like the old days.
DANIELLE	Ummm...a long smoldering ember about to burst into flame.

KELLY tears open her envelope.

KELLY	Save it for your "soap" Danny. I promised the baby-sitter I'd be home by twelve.
BOBBY	Quelle drag. We got a lot of old times to talk over.

DANIELLE   Hey, don't sweat it. We'll go over. The kid'll be
             comatose by now anyway.

KELLY   Nah, I can't ask you to do that for me.

DANIELLE   No big deal. The male population out there tonight is
             dismal, present company excepted, and Linda and I
             could use the time to work on the song — for
             tomorrow.

KELLY   Danielle, you know I can't come tomorrow.

DANIELLE   Jenny can take care of the kid.

KELLY   I can't afford two baby-sitters in one week.

BOBBY   If it's just a question of paying a baby-sitter...

KELLY   I pay my own way, Bobby.

DANIELLE   What'd you win, Kelly?

KELLY   A free colour consultation at Cherie Esthetics! How
             about you, Linda?

LINDA   Ah, I don't know. I didn't look yet.

KELLY   Well look, look.

             *KELLY picks up LINDA's envelope off the
             table, opens it and hands LINDA the certificate
             inside. LINDA looks at DANIELLE, a hint of
             desperation in her eyes.*

LINDA   Gee that's great...Look at what I got Danielle!

             *LINDA thrusts the certificate at DANIELLE who
             reads it.*

DANIELLE   You got a colour consultation too! Gee, we all got a
             colour consultation.

             *DANIELLE puts all three gift certificate together
             and hands them to KELLY.*

DANIELLE   You're winter. You're fall. I'm summer and we can
             bribe the baby-sitter with these. "A perfect gift for
             any occasion." Deal?

KELLY   (*laughs*) Deal.

             *DANIELLE laughs, grabs LINDA by the sleeve
             and starts to exit.*

DANIELLE   Have a good time, Kelly.

LINDA   Yeah, don't do anything I wouldn't do.

DANIELLE   Linda! We want the girl to have some fun.

             LINDA pokes her. DANIELLE laughs.

KELLY   I'll be home by two.

DANIELLE   Right. But just in case, I'll sleep over.

             As they leave, LINDA whispers to DANIELLE.

LINDA   Thanks, Danielle.

DANIELLE   God Linda, what do you do when I'm not around?

LINDA   Tell people I forgot my glasses.

DANIELLE   It's not that hard. Colour Consultation. C-o-l-o-u-r,
             Con, C-o-n-

             They exit.

KELLY	So?
BOBBY	So, you still remember "I Been Around"?
KELLY	You still do "I Been Around"?
BOBBY	Hell, I play them all. Come on.

BOBBY grabs KELLY by the hand and leads her back on stage..

KELLY	Twelve bar in E, boys.
BOBBY	"I Been Around".
KELLY	One, two, three, four...

They sing "I've Been Around" — both a bit amazed at how good they still sound together.

I'VE BEEN AROUND

B. & K.
I've been around, ooh baby I've been around
I've been around, ooh baby I've been around
But when it comes to lovin'
There ain't no better man that can be found

B. & K.   I've been around
BOBBY   I'm not the newest face in this town
B. & K.   I've been around
BOBBY   The older the goodie
The softer the sweeter the sound
B. & K.   And if you need me baby
Just gimme a call
And baby doll I'll come around

B. & K.
I've been around,
Ooh baby he's been around
I've been around
Ooh baby he's been around
But when it comes to lovin'
BOBBY   There ain't no better man that can be found

BOBBY	I've been down to the beach
KELLY	Been round the block
BOBBY	Been round the world
B. & K.	And that made some people talk
BOBBY	I've been thrown out of windows By some real angry men But the ladies just keep askin'
KELLY	When you comin' back again I've been around Been over and up and under and down
B. & K.	I've been around
BOBBY	I'm a silver fox, a killer, a thriller, a hound
B. & K.	Oh when it comes to lovin'
BOBBY	There ain't no better man that can be found

KELLY laughs. Blackout.

Act One, Scene Two

BOBBY and KELLY sit at a table with a nearly empty bottle between them. BOBBY's playing guitar. On the bandstand STAN — a big tumbler of scotch by his side — is playing along with BOBBY.

BOBBY
Darlin' I know I talk big
And I swagger a bit when I'm stoned
But nothin' is ever just what it seems
Behind the mask I'm scared and alone

KELLY joins in.

BOTH
All I've got left are dreams
All I've got in my pockets are memories
You're all that stands between me and the end
And all I've got left are my dreams

BOBBY
And it still sounds like a hit.

KELLY
Not exactly "new country" is it?

BOBBY
No, back then we were recording *real* country. I still don't understand how you could go from that to singing metal garbage.

KELLY
Just trying to make a buck, Bobby.

BOBBY
I'll drink to that. Damn we sound good together.

KELLY   Right.

BOBBY   I mean it.

KELLY   If I had a dime for every singer who tried that line on me...

BOBBY   Hey! You are forgetting that I am the first singer who ever tried that line on you.

KELLY   Right.

BOBBY   And it worked!

KELLY   (*laughing*) Anybody ever tell you you were the lowest kind of macho, tavern slug-slime?

BOBBY   (*like John Wayne*) Well, every once in awhile the guys in the band question my sense of style, but...

KELLY   The "chicks" still love it?

BOBBY   Hey. It's 1995. I don't call my female admirers "chicks" anymore.

KELLY   No? What do you call them?

BOBBY   Occupational hazards.

KELLY   You ever stop to consider that those "hazards" might have real feelings for you?

BOBBY   I have had some "serious relationships" you know.

KELLY   Yeah, but how long did they last?

BOBBY   Oww!

KELLY   Come on. Talk. Longest relationship.

BOBBY   Three years. Her name was Cathy. Left me for a parole officer. You done any better?

KELLY   Brian. Three and a half years. 'Course, he disappeared for seven months when I was pregnant forcing me to divorce him.

BOBBY   Those seven months don't count. I beat you.

KELLY   Guess we both know how to pick 'em, huh?

BOBBY   Guess I should mumble something about waiting for the right woman to come along.

KELLY   Right, then you look deep into my eyes and sigh.

BOBBY looks deep into her eyes and sighs.

BOBBY   The truth is the closest I ever came was with you.

KELLY   Right. I remember. What was her name? Darlene? Arlene?

BOBBY   Actually it was Darlene *and* Arlene.

They laugh.

KELLY   God, you were a son of a bitch.

BOBBY   I was young and stupid and you were no saint either. Remember that time Reveen came through town?

KELLY laughs and clinks glasses with BOBBY. They drink — a pause.

BOBBY   So tell me about the kid.

KELLY   Not much to tell. She's a good kid. I love her.

BOBBY   Well, come on, come on, where's the baby picture?

KELLY	You really want to see her?
BOBBY	Of course I do. I love the little ankle-biters.

KELLY shows him a picture.

KELLY	Amanda. She's bigger than that now.
BOBBY	She's a lucky kid.
KELLY	Why?
BOBBY	Heck, she's already got more hair than her dad.

KELLY laughs. BOBBY hands back the photo.

BOBBY	And she's got you.
KELLY	Right.
BOBBY	I wish you'd stop saying that! "Right". "Right"... People change you know? I'm tired of waking up wondering who I'm sleeping with. I'm tired of "buy the band a beer week" and playing to half-empty houses and...aw forget it. The only reason I'm getting into all this is that singing with you tonight made it feel good again.
KELLY	Right.
BOBBY	Don't you "right" me. There is no way you are going to stay out of this business.
KELLY	Want to bet?

Pause. They listen to STAN playing the song in the background.

BOBBY	Always figured you were too tough to ever quit on anything.

KELLY	You've got to pick your fights, Bobby. The kid came along. The husband went away. "Tits up in Wawa", right?
BOBBY	Miss it?
KELLY	Not really.
	STAN passes out face first into the piano.
BOBBY	Goodnight Stanley. (*pause*) So why now?
KELLY	What?
BOBBY	You came home but avoided this club a year. Why'd you show up tonight?
KELLY	No special reason. Just doin' a favour for a friend.
BOBBY	Nothing to do with me?
KELLY	Coming tonight or staying away?
BOBBY	Same thing isn't it?
KELLY	It's got dick to do with you Bobby.
BOBBY	Right.
KELLY	(*pause*) OK , I just needed to be up there again. Damn it all, some nights I lie in bed and it's like I can feel the heat of a follow spot burning into me. And I hear bottles poundin' on tables and people cheering and calling my name...standing up there knowing you can do something every person in that bar wants to do and can't. Sure, I miss it. I miss it like crazy.
BOBBY	Well, welcome home, babe.

> *BOBBY leans over to kiss KELLY, but she pulls back.*

KELLY   I'm not going to get hurt, Bobby. Never again.

BOBBY   I wouldn't do that to you.

KELLY   I wouldn't let you do that to me. Right?

> *They kiss. Blackout.*

Act One, Scene Three

*Afternoon. The bar is closed. The band is
working on "Friends". We hear the first few lines
of the song in the black, then lights up on the
scene. BOBBY paces the club, listening to
DANIELLE who is being backed by LINDA and
the band. STAN has a bottle perched beside him
on the piano. DANIELLE sings*

DANIELLE   (*singing*) To kiss away the teardrops and say; "Hey, it's all right"
And if you need a friend...

(*losing the time*) Five six seven eight...

(*singing again*) I'll be your friend tonight.

BOBBY   No, no, no, no, no.

LINDA   It's the phrasing, right Bobby?

BOBBY   That's right on the money, Linda. You've got to keep behind the beat.

DANIELLE   I am trying, Bobby.

KELLY enters from the washroom.

BOBBY   I know, and you're a powerhouse, but the feeling still isn't there and we've only got a week until the semi-final. Kelly, sing it for her again.

KELLY   (*sings*) I'll be your friend tonight.

DANIELLE   (*sings*) I'll be your friend tonight.

BOBBY   Beautiful. Let's take a break.

The band breaks. BOBBY exits. LINDA picks up a guitar and starts noodling around. HOSS comes over with his cards.

HOSS   Hey, Linda — you ever play Fish?

The band laughs.

LINDA   Yeah sure, when I was a kid.

HOSS winks at them.

HOSS   Want to play?

LINDA   I don't remember the rules.

HOSS   I'll teach ya. It's a good game, but tricky.

LINDA laughs. HOSS beams.

LINDA   Tell you what; why don't you help me with this song instead? It's a duet. Me and my daddy were workin' on it, but it never got finished.

HOSS   Okay.

As LINDA plays, KELLY and DANIELLE pick up on the new song. They come in on the second chorus.

(OLD TIME) LOVE, LOVE, LOVE

LINDA   The fridge is broke, hasn't worked in weeks
             The rent's past due and the roof it leaks
             I don't care, you are my turtle dove
             And all we need is love, love, love

HOSS   Like Loretta and Conway...George and Tammy!

LINDA   I got lovin' in my heart for you
             Honey there ain't nothing
             That I wouldn't do
             I'd dive into a hurricane
             To prove my love is true
             I got lovin' in my heart for you

LINDA   Help me Hoss!

             HOSS joins in, finding his way around the
             chorus and picking up on the more obvious last
             line.

LINDA   We got lovin' in the morning
             Lovin' every (*add HOSS*) night
             Love for all occasions
             So honey hold me (*add HOSS*) tight
             And love, love, love
             Will make it (*add HOSS*) right

THE GIRLS   I got lovin' in my heart for you
             Honey there ain't nothing
             That I wouldn't do

LINDA   I can't live without it
             It's crazy but it's true

HOSS   I love Jesus
             And baby I love you.

ALL   I love Jesus
             And baby I love you.

             They finish. Everybody howls and claps. HOSS
             can't believe it. BOBBY returns with a briefcase.

HOSS   Hey Bobby, me and Linda just wrote a song. Like the
             Kendalls. You hear?

BOBBY   Yup.

LINDA   What do you think?

BOBBY   That old-time music just doesn't sell anymore. What do you think Stan?

> *STAN has hauled out an accordian and is slipping it on.*

STAN   How about a Cajun feel?

> *HOSS looks hurt*

LINDA   A Cajun feel? Aw gee, Stan I don't know. Bobby?

BOBBY   I like it. Grab your fiddle we is gonna make some gumbo stew.

> *LINDA grabs a fiddle. BOBBY counts in the song playing with a Cajun feel. The others join in. HOSS rushes behind the bar and comes up with a grater and some spoons — instant percussion.*

(SWAMP) LOVE, LOVE, LOVE

LINDA   This old world is a funny place
We got trash TV. We got junk in space
We got lots but we all want more
We all go loco at the super store.

Lots of people got lots of things
Got great big houses, got diamond rings
We got nothing but the stars above
A simple song and love, love, love

THE GANG   I got lovin' in my heart for you
Honey there ain't nothing
That I wouldn't do
I would dive into a hurricane
To prove my love is true
I got lovin' in my heart for you

We got lovin' in the morning
Lovin' in the night
Love for all occasions
So honey hold me tight!

LINDA   And love will make it right

I got lovin' in my heart for you
Honey there ain't nothing
That I wouldn't do
I can't live without it
It's crazy but it's true
I love Jesus and I love you.

ALL   I got lovin' in my heart for you
Honey there ain't nothing
That I wouldn't do
I can't live without it
It's crazy but it's true
I love Jesus and I love you.
I love Jesus and I love you.
I love Jesus
And baby I love you.

LINDA   That's great! Thanks, Bobby.

BOBBY   That's my job, darlin'.

BOBBY opens his briefcase and takes out three contracts. He passes them to the girls.

BOBBY   OK, listen up. Remember those contracts I was talking to you about? I got them back from the lawyer today. Everybody take a look. I'm covering all the bases; manager, booker, arranger, publisher....

KELLY   I told him to put everything in black and white so we'll all know what to expect and so will he.

> *LINDA nods sagely, flipping through the
> document without being able to read it.*

LINDA   Ah...well...Hell of a lot of paper here isn't there?

KELLY   It's all pretty standard stuff. Bobby gets fifteen
percent and books Daddy's Girls exclusively.
Considering that my last manager wrote our contract
on the back of a table napkin, these are excellent.

> *LINDA scans it for a moment then hands it back
> to DANIELLE.*

LINDA   What do you think?

> *DANIELLE flips through LINDA's contract
> without really paying much attention.*

DANIELLE   Where do we sign — that's what I think.

BOBBY   Page twenty-six.

> *DANIELLE distracts the others from LINDA's
> clumsy penmanship by doing her best imitation
> of Ed Norton getting ready to sign his name.*

DANIELLE   Danielle Delores DuCharme — Chanteuse and —
watch out Wynona — Linda McGee.

> *DANIELLE takes LINDA's signed contract and
> hands it to BOBBY.*

BOBBY   OK. Starting next week I'm booking Daddy's Girls
right here at The Horseshoe. We'll build up a local
following plus give you all the confidence you need
to ace the contest.

> *DANIELLE loves it.*

DANIELLE	That's great Bobby, and you know, I've been thinking about our image...
KELLY	Here it comes.
DANIELLE	I see spangles, skin tight cat-suits, beaucoup la cleavage...
LINDA	Hell-bunnies-in-heat. No way.
DANIELLE	Why not? We need something for the audience to go nuts about.
LINDA	But I'm not sexy.
DANIELLE	You are sexy as hell. Look, we're good Linda and we "got soul" but there's nothing wrong with a bit of umph. I mean, I sure as hell don't want to get up on stage and be ignored. Stanley, give me that nice big D minor chord.

> *STAN does as he's told. DANIELLE sings the lead on "You've Got To Have A Gimmick".*

YOU'VE GOT TO HAVE A GIMMICK

DANIELLE
Well they say that country music
Is made by simple folks
But if you've been to Nashville
You know that is a joke.

Cause when it comes to pushin' product
There's no flies on those suits
Who sit around at RCA
In gold tipped cowboy boots

They dress you up in rhinestones
They dress you down in jeans
They change the way you talk
They video your dreams

(*spoken*) Help me out here girls

You gotta have a gimmick.
You gotta have a style
Have that something special
That drives the people wild
Listen to me angel, you sing just like a bird
But if you don't have a gimmick
You never will get heard

So gimme, gimme, gimme, gimme
Gimme, gimme, gimme that gimmick
Gimme, gimme, that gimmick
And I'll give you
A country music singing star.

> *DANIELLE keeps singing, but mike in hand*
> *hops off the stage and plays the song to HOSS,*
> *taking his hat, then acting out a little gun fight*
> *that results in HOSS getting shot.*

Now Billy Rae's got the "Achey Breaky"
And everybody's wearing hats
Lori leaves the lights on
And the Gambler's standin' pat.

But Hank he got the Lonesome Blues
Kitty had a heart of gold
Patsy she's got that achin' voice
They don't need gimmicks. They got soul

But now you gotta have a gimmick.
You gotta have a style
Got to have that something special
That drives the people wild
Listen to me angel, you sing just like a bird
But if you don't have a gimmick
You never will get heard

Gimme, gimme, gimme,
Gimme, gimme, gimme, that gimmick
You need a gimmick
To become a country music singing star

Gimme, gimme, gimme,
Gimme gimme that gimmick
You need a gimmick
To become a country music singing star

(*spoken*) Follow me guys.

You need a gimmick
To become a country music singing star.

> *BOBBY buttons the song. HOSS and the whole band hoot. DANIELLE wins this round. Blackout.*

Act One. Scene Four

BOBBY is on stage singing "Lay That Money Down".

LAY THAT MONEY DOWN

BOBBY
Well I rolled into a roadhouse
It was twenty-five past one
I was feeling sort of lonesome
And looking for some fun
Oh lord she was a beauty
Just a little on the trash side
I ordered up a jug of beer
And I bought that gal a rye

When the lights came up at half-past two
That gal still looked all right
So I hit her with a puppy dog smile
Said; You want to spend the night?

She said; "Lay that money down, Mister"
Lay that money down
We ain't going nowhere
'till you lay that money down

She said; "Lay that money down, Mister"
Lay that money down
I'll do anything for cash
If you lay that money down

I was playing in this Honky Tonk
Just outside Montreal
Everybody dressed in cowboy boots
And a moose head on the wall
Well this lumberjack he staggered up
He stood 'bout eight feet tall

He said; "Eh, you play 'Feelings'
Or you will not live to see last call".

Well I looked down at his fist
It looked like a wrecking ball
I'll play you any song you want
'Cause hell we know them all.

But you got to "Lay that money down, Monsieur"
Lay that money down
We ain't playing bullshit
'Till you lay that money down

"Lay that money down, Mister"
Lay that money down
I'll play anything for cash
So lay that money down

> *BOBBY hops off stage and moves on to the
> dance floor, getting HOSS involved in the
> action. This is a much loved, much rehearsed
> routine in which HOSS and BOBBY act out the
> lyrics of the song.*

BOBBY   There's a dive in Kapuskasing
That they call The Crippled Crow
The clientele is crazy
And the management is low
We played all week and was packin up
When the boss said;

HOSS   "Sorry Joe
We'd like to pay you off tonight
But we just don't have the dough"

BOBBY   I backed him up against the bar
I grinned at him real slow
Said; You're gonna pay us out tonight
Or to hell you're gonna go.

> *HOSS faints away in mock terror. Then laughs
> and waves at the crowd to let them know he's
> really OK. BOBBY climbs back on stage.*

You'd better; "Lay that money down, Mister"
Lay that money down
We ain't going nowhere
'till you lay that money down

"Lay that money down, Mister"
Lay that money down
You know that I would kill for cash
You better lay that money down
You ain't going nowhere
'till you lay that money down
You ain't going nowhere
'till you lay that money down

BOBBY   Thank you. And we'll be right back with the next
contestants in The Cross Canada Country Talent
Countdown semi-finals; "Daddy's Girls".

*The band plays a tag. BOBBY gets off the stage
and crosses to the table. HOSS hurries up to
him, picking up on his nervous vibe.*

HOSS   Geeze, Bobby. Something's the matter, isn't it?

BOBBY   We got trouble, Hoss.

HOSS   What. What?

BOBBY   "Daddy's Girls" are going to lose tonight.

HOSS   Oh no. They loved me doin' "Bud The Spud", didn't
they? Everybody loves that song 'cause it's about
potatoes. I'll drop out.

BOBBY   I'm not worried about "Bud The Spud" Hoss.

HOSS   Peg-Leg then? He remembered all the words to his
song tonight and he plays guitar too! People were
clapping real loud.

BOBBY   Hoss, the song's in C, he plays in D and sings in
B...People were clapping 'cause he was leaving.

HOSS   Yeah, he sucked. Who then Bobby? Who's gonna
beat "Daddy's Girls".

BOBBY	The Goddamn Elvis impersonator! Think, think, think.
HOSS	I am, Bobby.
BOBBY	Not you Hoss. Me.
HOSS	Me too, Bobby.

> *Lights up on the dressing room. LINDA is standing in front of a mirror looking at herself in profile. She has on a skin tight red dress, low-cut and slinky. DANIELLE is in a cat-suit, and KELLY in a great fringed dress. DANIELLE zips LINDA into her outfit.*

LINDA	'This thing is tight as a mosquito's ass stretched over a box car'.
KELLY	I beg your pardon?
LINDA	That's what Tex would have said.
DANIELLE	He'd love it.
LINDA	I don't even recognize myself.
DANIELLE	Believe me, it's an improvement. Right, Kelly?

> *DANIELLE starts working on LINDA's hair.*

KELLY	Incredible.
LINDA	(*sings*) "There ain't nothing like a friend." Come on sing it. "There ain't nothing like a friend..."
DANIELLE	Will you stop? We know the song.
LINDA	Well, I've got to do something 'til we go on.

KELLY   Relax. Bobby did his job. We are tighter than that
               insect's derriere. Jesus Danielle, take it easy!

DANIELLE   She's got to look hot, Kelly.

               DANIELLE pours herself a big glass of vodka.

KELLY   There's nothing hot about helmet hair.

               *DANIELLE polishes off her vodka and pours
               another.*

DANIELLE   It looks great.

KELLY   On the bride of Frankenstein it would look great, and
               you should watch how much you're drinking.

DANIELLE   The whole gang from Cherie is out there tonight. I
               got to be up.

KELLY   If you start to shoop when we're supposed to doop
               I'm gonna have your ass.

               DANIELLE laughs.

DANIELLE   She needs more drama.

               DANIELLE hauls out a tube of lipstick.

KELLY   Danielle! Not the pink frost!

DANIELLE   Yes, the pink frost. It's back — with a vengeance.

               *KELLY grabs for the lipstick. DANIELLE
               jumps away and starts shadow boxing.*

DANIELLE   Get back, get back. I'm a trained professional and I'm
               not afraid to use this.

               They spar, laughing.

LINDA   Will you two cut it out! I'm rattled enough already!

DANIELLE   Rattled? There's nothing to get rattled about. You've done this a million times, right Kelly?

KELLY   Right.

DANIELLE   A piece of cake, right?

KELLY   Right. Gimme a hit.

               KELLY takes a big slug from DANIELLE's bottle.

LINDA   Tell the truth. We're all petrified.

DANIELLE   OK, OK. Inside I'm Alpha-ghetti.

KELLY   Me too, but there's nothing you can do about that.

LINDA   Sure there is. Come on. Hold hands.

DANIELLE   What?

LINDA   Hold hands.

DANIELLE   You've been watching *Partridge Family* re-runs again.

LINDA   Tex and me used to do this anytime he had a big gig. Come on, what are you afraid of?

KELLY   Ah, what the hell, if it worked for Shirley Jones.

               They all hold hands.

LINDA   Now we all make a wish.

KELLY   Right Jiminy, where's the star?

LINDA   What do you want most, Danielle?

DANIELLE   I want to walk through the Mall on Monday and have everybody look at me and say, "There's Danielle. She's a singer."

LINDA   Kelly?

KELLY   OK. I wish...I want this to work. If this works I can get out of the Can Car Plant and still make a decent living for me and my kid. That's all.

DANIELLE   Linda?

LINDA   I wish that we do real good tonight and that we go on to win the national contest and that the three of us keep singing together until we are as old as The Carter Sisters. Now sing...one, two, three...

ALL   (*they sing*) "There ain't nothing like a (*out of key*) friend".

   They stop, totally horrified, then laugh.

LINDA   Get out of here! Both of you.

KELLY   I need a Southern Comfort.

DANIELLE   I want something with an umbrella in it.

   In the dressing room, LINDA sits alone re-doing her makeup.

LINDA   Daddy. I'm going out there in a minute and I'm going to get up on that stage and sing a song I "wrote" and all I can do is sit in here and feel like some kind of a cheat. I mean, I had to get Danielle to put the damn thing down on paper 'cause I can't even spell the words!

   All I see in this world are shapes Daddy, and colours, and I got to remember so much more than everybody else and hide all the time and I get so scared...That's why I want you to be with me on stage tonight. And I want you to be good, OK? And then I'll be good too. I love you.

DANIELLE and KELLY re-enter.

DANIELLE   (*singing*) I'll be your friend tonight.

KELLY   No, no.
(*sings*) I'll be your friend tonight.

DANIELLE   (*joining in*) ...friend tonight. Thank you very much.

BOBBY knocks on the door.

DANIELLE   *Entrez.*

BOBBY enters.

BOBBY   OK, listen up, nobody's going to like what I've got to say, but I'm your manager so I've got to say it. You are going to lose tonight.

DANIELLE   What?

BOBBY   This Elvis impersonator got up last set...

KELLY   We're going to lose to an Elvis impersonator!

BOBBY   He's got one of those white jump-suits. People went nuts.

DANIELLE   Come on, Bobby, there must be something we can do.

BOBBY   There is, but I can't ask you to do it.

DANIELLE   Screw it. Whatever it takes to win.

BOBBY   You mean that, Danielle?

DANIELLE   Of course I mean it. What do we have to do?

BOBBY   Kelly's got to sing "Friends".

DANIELLE   What?

BOBBY   Look Danielle, you are acing every other number in the act, but "Friends" is the money song.

KELLY   Bobby, don't do this.

BOBBY   Kelly, you can sell the song and we can't take a chance, not tonight. It's the semi-finals. We win, we can go all the way. We lose and it's all over.

DANIELLE   (*hurt and looking for support*). Linda?

LINDA   Ah...well...I don't know...I mean...Bobby's only been working on my songs for two weeks and they're sounding so good and...and ...if he says...we should try it...

         DANIELLE is devastated.

BOBBY   You're a smart kid Linda. (*to all of them*) And none of you will regret this.

         BOBBY exits.

LINDA   Danny I'm...Sorry.

         DANIELLE won't look at LINDA. LINDA exits.

KELLY   Danielle?

         KELLY tries to take DANIELLE's arm. She pulls away.

KELLY   Look Danielle, if this was up to me I'd say forget it but...It's Linda's song and...

DANIELLE   Linda would still be singing in your kitchen if it wasn't' for me.

KELLY   I know that, but...Jesus, Danielle you can't blame her for siding with Bobby.

DANIELLE   I've been wiping snot off her nose since she was thirteen years old and she's only known Bobby a couple of weeks!

KELLY   This isn't about loyalty. It's about business. Bobby's judgment...

DANIELLE   Bobby this! Bobby that! We both know why he's doing this and it's got nothing to do with judgment.

KELLY   What's that mean?

DANIELLE   It means every time he looks at you his pants melt off. First it's going to be this song, then it's going to be another...

KELLY   That's not going to happen.

DANIELLE   I worked for this. I found you and got you singing with me and Linda and I got you off your butts and down to this club and...It's just not fair!

KELLY   Fine. We both owe you. You want to sing the song I'll back off. But if Bobby's right, and you get up there and we lose...

Realizing what she's saying, KELLY stops herself.

KELLY   Sorry. I've no right to say that. You do it. I'll sing back-up.

A long painful moment.

DANIELLE   No. You sing it.

> *DANIELLE stands and heads for the stage.*
> *KELLY follows. BOBBY is on stage with the*
> *band. LINDA is waiting nearby. Seeing KELLY*
> *and DANIELLE, he goes into the intro for the*
> *song.*

BOBBY   (*playing Emcee to the hilt.*) All right! I'm back. How
about that Jerome "Little Elvis" Padrowski, eh? (*sung*
to the tune of "Suspicious Minds")

"He's caught in a trap. He can't get out,
Because his jump suit zipper's broken"

OK, our final contestants are three beautiful, talented
young ladies who I think are headed for the top. Let's
hear it for them — Kelly, Linda, and Danielle.
Daddy's Girls!

> *BOBBY goes into his intro and Daddy's Girls*
> *come on. They look hot and honky as all-get-out*
> *and hit the song right on cue. It's executed with*
> *real skill, complete with lighting effects and*
> *choreography.*

(THERE AIN'T) NOTHING LIKE A FRIEND

KELLY   Yeah we're fightin, the way we always do
And he's been drinking so tonight I'm callin' you
Sometimes you need somebody
Who can help your heart to mend.
When you're hurtin'there ain't nothing like a friend

You are his best friend
And you know I love him too
But sometimes baby, love can't pull you through
You know I get so restless
Thinkin' that no hope's in sight
Then I need somebody just like I need you tonight.

There ain't nothing like a friend
And I can't tell you why.
There ain't nothing like a friend
To hold you when you cry

To kiss away the teardrops
And say; "Hey it's all right"
And if you need a friend
I'll be your friend tonight.

And tomorrow is just another day
Same as always I'll be on my way
And I'll say " I owe you honey"
As I slip out your back door
And then you'll smile and say;
"Oh baby, that's what friends are for."

There ain't nothing like a friend
And I can't tell you why
There ain't nothing like a friend
To hold you when you cry

There ain't nothing like a friend
To say; "Hey it's all right"
There ain't nothing like a friend
And I'll be your friend tonight

The song ends. The girls do a bow The Supremes
would be proud of. This is a winning
performance. BOBBY looks at HOSS who is
whistling and applauding like mad. He gives him
a thumbs up. Blackout.

End of Act One.

Act Two, Scene One

*The bar. In the black. We hear an instrumental
version of "All I've Got Left Is Dreams".*

BOBBY   One, two, three, four...

*The song goes uptempo. It's now new country.
Lights up on the bar. Daddy's Girls are on stage
with BOBBY. — a slick act with well-
choreographed moves and a sense of confidence
that suggests time has passed. HOSS stands off
to one side watching the action, beer case under
his arm. KELLY's out front but DANIELLE
grabs attention by draping herself all over
BOBBY as he plays his solo. BOBBY plays up
the flirtation, oblivious to KELLY's growing
anger.*

ALL I'VE GOT LEFT IS DREAMS

THE GIRLS   All I've got left are dreams
All I've got in my pockets are memories
You're all that stands between me and the end
And all I've got left are my dreams

KELLY   I know that everyone's hurtin'
It seems that dreams just never come true
They're all made of sand
They just slip through your hands
But I'm gonna gamble all my dreams on you

THE GIRLS　　All I've got left are dreams
　　　　　　　　All I've got in my pockets are memories
　　　　　　　　You're all that stands between me and the end
　　　　　　　　And all I've got left are my dreams

　　　　　　　　　　BOBBY joins in trading lines with KELLY.

K & B　　　　I know love doesn't play the game
　　　　　　　　By any set of rules
　　　　　　　　But love can't be denied
　　　　　　　　By beggars or by fools

BOBBY　　　　Darlin' I can't help but love you
　　　　　　　　With you by my side I can win

B & K　　　　We'll forget the past, 'cause it never lasts
　　　　　　　　Together we'll never be lonesome again

ALL　　　　　We've got to follow our dreams
　　　　　　　　Or we'll end up lost in memories
　　　　　　　　You're all that stands between me and the end
　　　　　　　　So we've got to follow our dreams

　　　　　　　　We've got to follow our dreams
　　　　　　　　Or we'll end up lost in memories
　　　　　　　　You're all that stands between me and the end
　　　　　　　　So baby let's follow our dreams
　　　　　　　　You're all that stands between me and the end
　　　　　　　　So baby let's follow our dreams

　　　　　　　　　　The song ends and DANIELLE gives BOBBY a
　　　　　　　　　　big kiss. KELLY glares at BOBBY, then heads
　　　　　　　　　　for the dressing room.

BOBBY　　　　Thank you and good night. One, two, three...

　　　　　　　　　　The band goes into "Bobbie's Bump".
　　　　　　　　　　DANIELLE and LINDA leave the stage and head
　　　　　　　　　　for the dressing room. BOBBY winds up the
　　　　　　　　　　extro and crosses to the bar, where HOSS is
　　　　　　　　　　standing.

HOSS　　　　　What's all the fuss, Bobby? Kelly looked ready to
　　　　　　　　fight.

BOBBY	She is driving me crazy, Hoss. One minute we're "in sync", you know? She's funny and hot and, damn it all, I even like the kid and then...Yesterday she bought a cookbook.
HOSS	Wow, Bobby! She's in love with you!
BOBBY	And came over to my place and cleaned up!
HOSS	She loves you for sure!
BOBBY	She threw out my entire collection of "Outlaw Biker".
HOSS	Even the "Tattooed Mama" issue?
BOBBY	Because of the "Tattooed Mama" issue. And every day it's, "Don't do this, don't do that". She's always on my case.
HOSS	(*worried*) You hate that, Bobby. Chicks get on your case...watch out. You're gone.
BOBBY	Wish it was still that simple.

HOSS has to think about that one.

HOSS	Yeah, it's not that simple...

Lights up on the dressing room. Action moves fluidly between playing areas. Tension crackles between KELLY and DANIELLE. LINDA, upset by the tense energy, strums her guitar.

LINDA	(*sings*) The first thing I remember My daddy sang to me Playing "Wildwood Flower" With a guitar on his knee. He sang "Movin' On", "Jambalaya" We were proud and free...

KELLY Linda will you lay off? All these song-ettes are driving me crazy.

HOSS How come?

DANIELLE What's your problem, Kelly?

BOBBY 'Cause I love her! At least I think I do.

KELLY You're my problem sweetheart.

    KELLY exits to washroom.

BOBBY Hell, I don't know.

HOSS Come on, Bobby, ya must know if you love her — 'cause of the way it feels.

BOBBY How's that?

HOSS All confused, like you don't know what to say or nothing and you're afraid, 'cause...Aw geeze, Bobby.

BOBBY Hoss, Hoss, Hoss.

HOSS Yeah, yeah, yeah.

BOBBY Linda? Now didn't I warn you?

HOSS Yeah, Bobby, but ...

BOBBY You're just gonna get hurt. Everybody gets hurt.

HOSS Can't help it. And I can't even tell her, 'cause...you know. (*pause*) Boy, women; "Can't live with 'em, can't live with 'em." Eh, Bobby?

    BOBBY laughs.

HOSS What we gonna do?

BOBBY   Well, guess I'll go in there and sing her a love song.
                Wish me luck.

HOSS   Luck, Bobby.

                *BOBBY picks up a newspaper from the bar and
                heads for the dressing room. HOSS sits there
                thinking hard.*

HOSS   Oh Linda I love you
                But I don't have the words
                And guess you could say I'm not smart

                No, no, can't say Linda, ah..."Honey, I love
                you"...Nah. "Baby, I love you." " Sweetheart, I love
                you". (*making a face, then thinks hard*)

                (*sings*) Oh darlin' I love you
                But I don't have the words
                And guess you could say I'm not smart

                (*pleased with his new lyric*) Oh, I don't know about
                that.

                *Lights shift to the dressing room. A knock on
                the door.*

DANIELLE   Come!

                *BOBBY enters the dressing room, full of false
                enthusiasm. As he speaks, KELLY re-enters.*

BOBBY   Hey! You see the review in the "Comical-Journal"?
                Frank loved you guys, so I faxed the article to Fraser
                over at the TV station. I've got him and the contest
                producer coming down tomorrow night to take a look
                at your act. You watch, I'm going to get you the
                closing spot on the final.

DANIELLE   I love this man!

DANIELLE hoots and hugs him.

KELLY   The closing spot? (*dryly*) Wow, Danielle — time to invest in that new push-up bra.

DANIELLE   What do you think, Bobby? Do I need a new push-up bra?

BOBBY   (*like Groucho*) You looked any hotter we'd all get arrested.

KELLY   Will you just cut it out!

DANIELLE   Come on Kel, we're just fooling around.

KELLY   Right. And Bobby's famous for fooling around.

BOBBY   Jesus, Kelly, relax.

KELLY   I don't feel very relaxed at the moment.

BOBBY   What did I do now?

KELLY   If you don't know, I can't help you.

BOBBY   Just spell it out, OK?

KELLY   You want to be with me?

BOBBY   Yeah.

KELLY   Then tell her to stop crawling all over you like some kind of...python in heat!

DANIELLE   Oh hiss.

BOBBY   For God's sake, Kelly! It's just part of the act.

KELLY   Well it sure doesn't look like an act to me and I've had just about all the hi-test testosterone I can take!

BOBBY   Sometimes you sound so much like a wife...

KELLY   Well I can solve that one — easy.

          KELLY starts to exit.

BOBBY   Kelly!

          BOBBY grabs KELLY's arm.

BOBBY   That's not what I meant.

          KELLY shakes free.

KELLY   I am not going to hang around humming "Stand By Your Man" while you run your numbers.

DANIELLE   (*sings*) But if you love him you'll forgive him...

KELLY   Bite it, Danielle.

          KELLY hurries out.

BOBBY   Kelly! You come back here!

          BOBBY exits.

LINDA   Danielle! Why are you being such a jerk?

DANIELLE   I'm a jerk? She's the one who pitched the fit.

LINDA   If you'd stop flirting with Bobby...

DANIELLE   He is flirting with me too!

LINDA   Kelly is your friend.

DANIELLE   Yeah, I think about that every time she steals another one of my songs.

LINDA   They're not your songs. They're our songs.

DANIELLE   I stand corrected.

LINDA   We're a group, remember?

DANIELLE   Sure, all for one and one for all!

LINDA   Daddy's Girls was your idea in the first place, Danny.

DANIELLE   Oh, you remember.

LINDA   Of course I remember!

DANIELLE   Then why do you always take her side?

LINDA   Aw Danielle, don't.

                 *LINDA picks up the paper and hands it to
                 DANIELLE.*

LINDA   Look, we're doing good. What'd they say?

DANIELLE   Read it yourself.

                 *DANIELLE drops the paper in front of LINDA
                 and walks out. LINDA bites her lip then strums
                 her guitar. DANIELLE crosses to the bar and sits
                 beside STAN. He slides her his drink. She
                 polishes it off and signals for more. HOSS takes
                 a deep breath and slips into the dressing room.*

LINDA   (*sings*) It was just a flat top box
                 The frets are all wore down
                 Not too much to look at
                 But I still can hear the sound
                 Of my Daddy singing
                 Sweet mountain harmony
                 My Daddy, his Gibson guitar and me

LINDA   (*she stops*) Aw hell.

HOSS	Hi Linda.
	LINDA smiles at HOSS.
LINDA	Hi Hoss.
HOSS	Thanks. What ya doin'?
LINDA	Just working on a song.
HOSS	Yeah...It's about your daddy, huh? .Where's it go next?
LINDA	I don't know.
	Pause. HOSS tries to cheer LINDA up.
HOSS	How 'bout...(*sings to her tune*) "I can still remember my Daddy's Nudie suit..." You know what a Nudie suits is?
LINDA	Sure, it's an outfit like Tex used to wear. The good ones all come from this tailor called Nudie...
HOSS	...who lives in Hollywood. Must have been neat growing up with a dad in a Nudie suit!
	LINDA laughs.
LINDA	I wish everybody was as easy to talk to as you Hoss.
HOSS	Bobby says I'm easy to talk to 'cause I don't get half of what people say, but he's just kiddin'. I understand everything pretty good. Ah...ah...like...Bobby is in love with Kelly and he's real scared 'cause Bobby never fell in love with hardly nobody and that's why she's mad at Danielle. And...and...that's all I know — for sure. Guess I don't know much about love. (*pause*) You ever fall in love, Linda? No, no,

geesh...I mean, I mean gosh...you know...How's your song go next?

LINDA   Not sure.

LINDA starts to strum.

HOSS   You got any words written down?

LINDA   Nah. I make 'em up in my head first.

HOSS   Me too. I make 'em up and then I tell Bobby and he writes 'em down and helps rhyme 'em and stuff.

LINDA   Yeah, I know.

HOSS   I got a new song too, all worked out, but I haven't sung it to Bobby...'cause I want you to do it with me.

HOSS   Here. You can write it down, OK?

HOSS hauls out a pad and pencil and puts it down in front of LINDA. She takes the pencil awkwardly.

HOSS   It goes; "I wait..."

LINDA pushes down hard snapping the pencil point

LINDA   Oh damn. I broke it.

HOSS takes the pencil.

HOSS   OK. Don't matter. I got my pencil knife.

HOSS gets out his knife and starts to carefully sharpen the pencil. BOBBY walks into the bar and gets a drink. DANIELLE crosses to him, abandoning STAN. He sighs and goes back to

the piano where he begins to softly play
"Nothing Like A Friend".

DANIELLE   So where's Kelly?

BOBBY   Half-way to Hibbing for all I know. I mean, God,
what did we do tonight, that was so much different
from any other night?

DANIELLE   Nothing. But you know what they say; the longer the
relationship, the shorter the leash.

BOBBY   Yeah, well, maybe I'm not quite ready to heel.

    DANIELLE clinks glasses with BOBBY. They
    drink.

BOBBY   Aw hell, I don't know.

DANIELLE   You love her?

BOBBY   Yeah, I think so, but sometimes it feels like a cage. I
start askin'; "Is this thing called *love* enough?"

DANIELLE   Sometimes. Other times you've got to let it go.

BOBBY   I mean, what does she want from me?

DANIELLE   A Bobby Curtis T-shirt?

    BOBBY laughs.

DANIELLE   You've got something wild inside you Bobby. That
scares some people. (*pause*) Me, I wouldn't like to
see it tamed. Anyway...

BOBBY   Anyway...

DANIELLE   Let's have another drink and give it a rest.
Tomorrow's another day right?

BOBBY   Thanks, Danielle.

DANIELLE   Hey, (*sings*) That's what friends are for.

> *DANIELLE reaches over and tilts BOBBY's hat*
> *down over his eyes.*

DANIELLE   Right, Dwight?

> *BOBBY stands and goes to the back bar to get*
> *drinks. In the dressing room HOSS hands*
> *LINDA the sharpened pencil.*

HOSS   There you go. Now. It says; "I wait every night"...

LINDA   I can't, Hoss.

HOSS   Why not?

LINDA   I just can't!

> *HOSS is suddenly hurt and afraid.*

HOSS   No, no, sorry...no need to fuss, if you don't want to..
it's just...just I wrote it 'cause...for you to like it. Oh
geeze. I...I got to go. Yeah. Gotta...

> *HOSS stands and starts to leave.*

LINDA   No wait, Hoss. I didn't mean to hurt your feelings.

HOSS   Oh you didn't hurt, Linda. I'm pretty brave you know.

LINDA   Yeah. Wish I was, then maybe I'd stick up for myself
when I should. (*pause*) Look Hoss I want to write
your song down for you but...

HOSS   What?

LINDA   If I say you've got to promise never to tell anybody.

HOSS	I promise.
LINDA	Hoss. I can't write your song down because I can hardly even write my own name.
HOSS	(*laughs*) Come on, Linda. You're smart.
LINDA	No I'm not, Hoss. I'm stupid. I can't read or write. I can just barely fake it.
HOSS	But...but...how come you can't write Linda? You go to school and all that?
LINDA	Not much, see, Tex and me traveled 'round all the time. He tried to teach me, but...you know.
HOSS	Didn't you learn your letters or nothing?
LINDA	Sure, but I'm just no good at putting them together.
HOSS	Well I could...I could teach you. I'm...I'm pretty good, sort of. Here...here.

HOSS takes the pad.

HOSS	I wait. That's I. Big one. And then W...E- no, A - T.. and...ah...

HOSS gets lost.

LINDA	Never mind that, Hoss. Let's just sing your song instead. Tell me how it goes. I'll catch on.

LINDA picks up her guitar.

HOSS	OK. It goes like ah...G, then...

HOSS hums a "C"

HOSS	And then you go up.

LINDA   C...and then...

> *LINDA strums the D 7th.*

LINDA   That it?

HOSS   Yeah, but like a waltz.

> *LINDA plays the structure.*

HOSS   Yeah. That's good.

> *As LINDA play,s the tune drifts into the bar.*
> *STAN, hears it and starts to play along. BOBBY*
> *and DANIELLE toast each other.*

BOBBY   Friends.

DANIELLE Friends.

> *They drink.*

DANIELLE You think I got any talent, Bobby?

BOBBY   Of course.

DANIELLE Then how come you keep on shoving me into the
              background?

BOBBY   It's not you, Danielle. It's the songs Linda's writing
              and my game plan for the group and a dozen other
              angles I've got to take into consideration.

DANIELLE It still hurts. (*pause*) You know, before I brought
              Kelly and Linda to the club? I use to come by with
              the girls from Cherie. Used to sit here and I always
              used to wish...ah, never mind.

BOBBY   No, what?

DANIELLE   I just always wanted to dance with you. You know?

BOBBY   Really?

DANIELLE   I'm a hell of a dancer, Bobby.

BOBBY   Come on.

>   *BOBBY stands, bows formally, takes
>   DANIELLE's hand and leads her on to the dance
>   floor. HOSS begins to sing; "I Wait and I Wait".
>   They begin to waltz — smooth, formal dancing.*

I WAIT AND I WAIT

HOSS   I wait every night for you to walk in the door
And you smile as you walk my way
I wait 'for the time when you get up on stage
'Cause your voice just takes me away

I wait and I wait
'til I can't wait no more
Then I smile as you walk out the door

Oh darlin', I love you
But I don't have the words
And guess you could say I'm not smart
I always thought love was a simple thing
But now it's just breakin' my heart.

And then I wait for tomorrow
When I'll see you again
And I swear this time I'll have my say
I'll tell you I love you
I swear every night
That tomorrow won't be like today

I waited all night
For you to walk in the door
And you smiled when you walked my way
I wait for the time you step up to the mike
And your voice just takes me away

I wait and I wait
Until I can't wait no more
And I smile as you walk out the door

> *HOSS stops, but STAN keeps playing and*
> *BOBBY and DANIELLE keep dancing. The dance*
> *is becoming more intimate as it goes on.*

LINDA   That was beautiful, Hoss.

> *HOSS looks down, suddenly too shy to reply.*

LINDA   Well, I better pack up on stage.

> *LINDA gets up.*

HOSS   Linda, just 'cause you don't write so good — that
don't mean nothin'. You're everyday folks is all. It's
everyday folks make the difference in life. And
ah...everybody's special in their own way, eh? (*a*
slight pause, HOSS doesn't want to talk in clichés)
But you're way more special than that!

LINDA   Thank you, Hoss.

> *LINDA gives HOSS a peck on the cheek. He's*
> *overwhelmed.*

HOSS   Linda.

LINDA   Yeah?

HOSS   (*pause*) Nothing.

> *LINDA exits to the stage. HOSS sings again.*

HOSS   I wait and I wait
Until I can't wait no more
And I smile as you walk out the door

BOBBY and DANIELLE are caught up in the moment. She pulls away from him for a second and smiles. A beat. She kisses him. He responds. They hold the kiss for a moment. KELLY walks into the bar and sees them.

KELLY   Right!

Blackout.

Act Two, Scene Two

BOBBY is on the pay phone listening to it ring on the other end. In the dressing room, LINDA and DANIELLE sit and worry. BOBBY hangs up.

HOSS You get her, Bobby?

BOBBY Nope. Look, send the bozos at table twelve another round on me, OK?

HOSS That's Mr. Fraser and the producer!

BOBBY Right, the suits.

HOSS rushes off to tell the bartender. BOBBY heads for the dressing room. Lights up on the dressing room.

DANIELLE All I did was kiss him.

LINDA Didn't you realize what would happen?

DANIELLE It was just a little kiss. Look...I wasn't thinking. I was feeling.

LINDA Well how are you feeling now?

DANIELLE To tell you the truth I am feeling pretty good.

DANIELLE looks in the mirror then re-does her lipstick. A knock on the door.

DANIELLE   Enter.

BOBBY   I couldn't get ahold of Kelly so we'll have to go on without her.

LINDA   But you've been pushing a trio with Kelly up front. That's what they're expecting to hear.

BOBBY   So we're going to surprise him.

LINDA   We sound awful without Kelly.

DANIELLE   No we don't! I can handle the material, Linda.

LINDA   Come on Danielle, you can't sing like Kelly and you know it!

DANIELLE   Thank you. Thank you. Thank you!

BOBBY   OK, can it. Danielle you'll sound great and we're going on with or without Kelly.

LINDA   But...

BOBBY   No buts, Linda. I'm not going to look like a fool in front of those producers, so get ready. I'll round up the band.

BOBBY exits. DANIELLE fusses with her make-up. LINDA is absolutely miserable.

LINDA   I won't do it.

DANIELLE   You are not going to wreck this showcase, Linda.

LINDA   No, you already did that.

DANIELLE   Look, do you want to be a songwriter?

LINDA   Well of course I do.

DANIELLE   Well more than anything else the producer is here to listen to your songs. Don't blow your chance because I made a mistake.

LINDA   Danielle, this isn't going to work.

DANIELLE   Look, just give me the same kind of chance you gave Kelly. Let me sing. You owe me that much Linda. You know you do.

LINDA   (*taking a breath*) Let's go.

> *DANIELLE and LINDA exit the dressing room. BOBBY and the band vamp on "Honky Tonk Queen".*

BOBBY   Hi, I'm Bobby C! Welcome to The Golden Horseshoe, home of next week's Cross Canada Country Countdown finals! In the audience tonight are the producer and sponsor of this momentous event; from CKPR TV right here in Thunder Bay, Mr. Douglas Fraser and sitting with Doug, all the way from Medicine Hat, Alberta, host of CHUD Broadcasting's "Spurs and Saddles", Jimmy "Big Boy" Jones. Let's hear it for them!

OK, now let's bring on the act these two good ol' boys are here to see, Ladies and Gentlemen, please give a very warm welcome to "Daddy's Girls".

> *DANIELLE struts on stage in her glory and ready to rock. LINDA follows. But at that very moment KELLY enters dressed in a new outfit and looking great. BOBBY sees her and breaks into a big smile.*

BOBBY   And now the star of Daddy's Girls — Kelly you're
         more important to me than anybody in this whole
         wide world. Let's hear it for her folks — Miss Kelly
         Connors!

         DANIELLE looks at LINDA, confused for a
         moment and then quickly slides away from the
         lead mike as KELLY takes the stage and sings.

HONKY TONK QUEEN

KELLY   You told me when we met
         You never had no one like me
         We had something special
         That lovers seldom see
         I woke up one morning
         And found out you were gone
         Oh yeah you're something special
         But you don't last very long

         You thought it was a joke
         A hit and run affair
         Well Babe you got me mixed up
         With somebody who might care
         Now I'll show you trouble
         Like you ain't never seen
         A wicked, wild, woman child
         A honky tonk queen

         I'm drinking double Jack
         I'm prowlin like a cat
         I'm up for anything
         And I just keep on coming back
         They say that I've gone bad
         That I'm evil and I'm mean
         Living fast and running crazy
         Hard to handle, easy lady
         Yeah, I am a Honky Tonk Queen

         I see you leaning there
         Like you're holding up the bar
         Givin' me them special eyes
         That once got you so far
         But I don't buy slip and sliding'
         And I'm gonna set you wise
         'Cause all you do is specialize
         In telling special lies.

I'm drinking double Jack
I'm prowlin like a cat
I'm up for anything
And I just keep on coming back
They say that I've gone bad
But I'm the best that's ever been
Living fast and running crazy
A hard to handle, easy lady
Yeah, I am a Honky Tonk Queen

I'm drinking double Jack
I'm prowlin like a cat
I'm up for anything
And I just keep on coming back
They say that I've gone bad
That I'm evil and I'm mean
Living fast and running crazy
A hard to handle, easy lady
Yeah, I am a Honky Tonk Queen

The song ends. Blackout. In the black we hear
Daddy's Girls, on tape, singing the last few lines
of "Friends", followed by enthusiastic applause.

Act Two, Scene Three

*KELLY sits in the bar. DANIELLE and LINDA
are in the dressing room. BOBBY enters and
crosses to KELLY.*

BOBBY   Well hell, Fraser loved Daddy's Girls and "Friends"
just cinched the closing spot on the contest. Didn't I
tell you!

BOBBY tries to kiss KELLY. She pulls away.

KELLY   Keep your hands off me, man.

BOBBY   Kelly listen. Last night when you walked out of that
dressing room I thought you were gone for good. I
was scared and angry and confused and Danielle...I
swear it will never happen again.

KELLY   It's too late, Bobby.

BOBBY   Kelly, listen, listen, keep working with me. I'll make
it up to you.

KELLY   No. I had to come in for the showcase because the
producers were here and I owe Linda that much but
...it's over. You got a week before the show. Find a
replacement.

BOBBY   Don't say it's over, Kelly. I'll do whatever you want
but...

KELLY   I can't do it. I will *never* get up on stage with
             Danielle again. It hurts too much.

             *BOBBY takes a long, deep breath, realizing what
             he's got to do and hating it.*

BOBBY   Right. Right. Right

             *BOBBY slowly walks to the dressing room.
             DANIELLE is nervously re-doing her make up.*

DANIELLE So I told you it was no big thing. I knew she'd show.

LINDA   Come on, Danielle. Kelly's crazy jealous. You've got
             to...

DANIELLE Kelly's a big girl. She can roll with the punches.
             Hell, me and Bobby...no way. So, I cornered Doug
             Fraser, out there. He loved the act...especially me
             and...

             There is a knock on the door.

LINDA   Come in.

             BOBBY enters.

BOBBY   Linda?

LINDA   Yeah?

BOBBY   They love "Friends". They love Kelly and they want
             to give us the closing spot on the show.

LINDA   Really? Great!

BOBBY   But there's a problem and we've got to deal with it.

LINDA   What?

BOBBY   Danielle. (*to DANIELLE*) I'm sorry but they had a
             lot of problems with your performance.

DANIELLE   Oh, cut the crap Bobby. Fraser loved me. It's Kelly,
             right?

BOBBY   All right. It's Kelly. She won't work with you.

DANIELLE   And?

BOBBY   Linda, we know "Friends" won't work without Kelly.

LINDA   What are you trying to say?

BOBBY   This is business Linda. Believe me I've been through
             every other possibility and they all work out the same
             Everybody loses.

DANIELLE   Say it to me, Bobby, not to her.

BOBBY   I'm sorry, Danielle. 'You're fired'.

DANIELLE   You bastard.

LINDA   You can't fire Danielle.

BOBBY   I just did.

LINDA   I said you can't fire Danielle! She's part of Daddy's
             Girls.

BOBBY   So is Kelly.

LINDA   Well then tell Kelly to come and talk to us. We'll
             sort it out, won't we Danielle?

BOBBY   It's too late for that. Kelly *will not* work with
             Danielle.

LINDA   Well then, that's it for Daddy's Girls.

BOBBY	No. Daddy's Girls is doing "Friends" in the contest. Even if it's just Kelly and a couple of back up singers.
LINDA	You can't do that.
BOBBY	Yes I can.
LINDA	Daddy's Girls doesn't exist without me and Danielle.
BOBBY	I own the name "Daddy's Girls". It's in your contract.

LINDA flounders for a moment.

BOBBY	I'm trying to do what's right for you, Linda. It's your song.
LINDA	I'll take my song and walk.
BOBBY	My publishing company controls the rights to all the songs we've registered — including "Friends".
LINDA	But...that's my song.
BOBBY	Read your contract again. Anything I publish I control. Period.

LINDA almost freezes up, but then her temper flares.

LINDA	Well to hell with you! And to hell with your contract and the contest and all the other bullshit you've pulled on us — you limp-dicked little son of a bitch!

BOBBY exits. LINDA is about to cry.

LINDA	He's gonna take everything.
DANIELLE	No. I'm not going to let that happen, Linda. If I have to get the boot...

LINDA   I'm not going to let him push you around.

DANIELLE   Don't you dare sacrifice your chance for me!

LINDA   I owe you.

DANIELLE   No. I won't let you run around picking up my mess
               like you did with Tex.

LINDA   What?

DANIELLE   I remember how you used to get his guitar out of
               hock every weekend and get him to the gig and take
               him home after and put him to bed. Well I'm not
               Tex!

LINDA   You're talking crazy.

DANIELLE   No, I'm not. You can't read because you never went
               to school and you didn't go to school because you
               spent your whole life taking care of that old drunk.

LINDA   Just shut up about my father!

DANIELLE   You blew your first chance for him and I will not let
               you blow this one by standing up for me. From now
               on you worry about yourself Linda and no one else.
               I'm out of here.

               *DANIELLE exits, pushing by HOSS who's been
               drawn by their fight.*

HOSS   Linda? What happened?

               LINDA doesn't answer.

HOSS   Ah...Ah...OK, OK no need to fuss, no need to fight.
               You want to play Fish? When I get the blues it
               makes me feel good and it's easy.

> *HOSS sits down and starts counting out cards, afraid to look up at LINDA.*

HOSS You get seven and I get seven and we put the rest down here. Them's the fish in the pond.

> *HOSS looks at his hand, still not looking at LINDA.*

HOSS Then you try and get cards all the same, but that can be hard so you got to ask for help.

> *LINDA starts to sob.*

HOSS Linda. What's the matter?

LINDA Bobby gave us bad contracts and stole my song and kicked Danielle and me out of Daddy's Girls!

HOSS Bobby wouldn't do that. He's my best friend.

LINDA He did it. Oh God Hoss. It's my fault...

> *LINDA cries. HOSS has no idea what to do, but after a moment he clumsily puts his arms around LINDA.*

LINDA I'm afraid.

HOSS You don't got to be afraid Linda. I won't let no one hurt you. They can't...'cause...'cause you're my girl and nobody hurts my girl...Just tell me and I'll make it better.

> *HOSS tries to kiss her. LINDA suddenly realizes what's happening and pulls away.*

LINDA Hoss!

HOSS   Geeze, Linda I didn't mean to...You was...I...you was
                cryin'.

                *HOSS backs off with an inarticulate groan and
                rushes out. Lights up on the bar. BOBBY sits
                talking softly to KELLY. They're both upset.
                HOSS comes rushing on.*

HOSS   Bobby. Bobby! BOBBY!!!

                *BOBBY stands and hurries towards HOSS, trying
                to calm him. KELLY watches, appalled.*

BOBBY   Hoss...

HOSS   Linda's crying, Bobby. She says...she says you hurt
                her. Bobby you got to fix it. Linda's cryin' and I-I-I...

BOBBY   Just stay out of it, Hoss.

HOSS   She says you're kickin' her out!

BOBBY   Nobody's kicking her out.

HOSS   But Linda said! She said you stole her song!

BOBBY   I didn't steal her song. I'm her publisher. My job is
                to make sure her work is properly represented. That's
                what I'm doing.

HOSS   But you fired her and Danielle.

BOBBY   Hoss, I had to fire Danielle. Linda quit.

HOSS   'Cause...'cause Danielle is her friend.

                *LINDA enters, unseen by HOSS, but KELLY
                sees her.*

BOBBY   Look, I'm sorry, but there's nothing I can do about it right now. So pick up some bottles, OK? I'll explain later.

                        BOBBY starts to walk away, but HOSS grabs him. It's a sudden violent move BOBBY isn't expecting.

HOSS   No!

BOBBY   Let go of me!

HOSS   No! You got to make Linda stop crying. You got to. You're my friend and I love her. I love her!

BOBBY   *(fighting him off)* Let go of me, you stupid retard!

HOSS   *(hurt and, for a moment, passive)* I'm not a retard. I'm slow is all.

BOBBY   I'm sorry, Hoss.

HOSS   You got to do what's right, Bobby. You got to give Linda back her song....or else!

BOBBY   I can't do that.

HOSS   Then you're not my damn friend anymore.

BOBBY   Then I guess I'm not your friend anymore.

                        HOSS turns and starts to walk away. Then looks at LINDA and realizes she's heard everything. LINDA takes a step towards him. He runs into the kitchen.

LINDA   Hoss, wait....

                        KELLY crosses to LINDA.

KELLY   Linda you've got this thing wrong — Bobby...

> *LINDA nearly slaps KELLY then rushes out.*
> *BOBBY crosses to KELLY and puts his arm*
> *around her. He notices STAN standing by the bar*
> *watching him.*

BOBBY   What are you looking at!

> *STAN looks down at his drink.*

STAN   Ice.

> *BOBBY and KELLY exit. STAN does the same.*
> *A long moment, then HOSS comes out of the*
> *kitchen. He crosses to the phone booth, drops in*
> *a quarter and punches zero.*

HOSS   Ah...hello. Hoss Cartright here. Hi Operator? I want
to talk to the TV guy is going to put on the Cross
Canada Talent Hunt. At home. Yeah he's...ah
Douglas Fraser and he's in White Oaks I think. 411?
Ah...I'm not too good at that you know. No, 'cause I
won't remember. Yeah...ah, can you dial it? Thank
you. Thanks and thanks for my quarter back.

> *HOSS takes the quarter out of the return slot.*

HOSS   Mr. Fraser? I got to talk with you about the contest.
(*pause*) Jerry Cartright here...Hoss, from the Golden
Horse..."Everybody's favourite singing cowboy".
Right. Hi, Hoss.(*pause*) Oh, what time is it anyway?
Oh. Sorry. Mr. Fraser this is real important. It's
about Daddy's Girls. You know Danielle? Danielle,
OK, she's not so good. Bobby kicked her and Linda
out of the band. Yeah, and Linda's song? She wrote it
and he's gonna keep it for the contest. Linda's got to
be in the contest so somebody's got to do
somethin'...'cause it's no fair! It's all 'cause of

Bobby's contracts and she can't even read *! (realizing he's spilled the beans)* Oh geeze!

HOSS looks at the phone in horror, then quickly hangs up. Blackout.

Act Two, Scene Four

> *In the bar. LINDA stands nervously playing "My
> Daddy, A Gibson Guitar And Me" on the guitar
> and looking very uncomfortable. HOSS stands
> fiddling with a video camera. DANIELLE sits on
> the edge of the stage working on STAN.*

DANIELLE   Come on Stan, we need you.

STAN   Danielle, I've been living in the store room for two
weeks and if I get chucked out of the band, I'll have
to pay my bar tab...

DANIELLE   Show some backbone, Stanley. You can't spend your
whole life hiding in a store room and pickled in J&B.

STAN   But if I get thrown out...

> *DANIELLE snuggles up.*

DANIELLE   I'd have to take you home with me.

STAN   I'm in.

DANIELLE   OK! Linda. Get up here, take a deep breath, smile and
sing.

STAN grabs a guitar as LINDA nervously goes to the mike. HOSS trains the camera on her and she freezes. A wooden smile is plastered to her face.

DANIELLE   Oh boy. OK. Just calm down Linda. And breathe. OK, so...Hoss, point the camera at me and start shooting.

HOSS   I been shooting.

LINDA   (*alarmed*) You have?

DANIELLE   Oh geeze. Ok, it doesn't matter. Just rewind to the top of the tape and we'll try it again.

HOSS   How you do that?

DANIELLE   You hit the rewind button.

HOSS looks at the camera trying to figure that out. DANIELLE sighs, then HOSS smiles.

HOSS   Never mind. Don't have to rewind...never turned it on.

HOSS laughs, turns the camera on and zooms in on LINDA.

HOSS   Close up on the star.

HOSS starts goofing around, peeking out from behind the lens and waving at LINDA, doing anything to make her laugh. Finally she cracks a smile.

DANIELLE   That's the stuff. Show time. Hoss!

HOSS focuses on DANIELLE and she plays to the camera.

DANIELLE   Hi Douglas. We must stop meeting like this. Listen I just want to thank you personally for letting Linda and I tape this audition for the contest. You're a sweetheart. So without further ado, here she is...Binda LeGee...Oh...Cut. Cut Hoss!

HOSS just keeps on shooting.

HOSS   No this is fun. Trust me!

DANIELLE   OK. (*she does a comic blither, then snapping out of it, she smiles*) Here she is — Linda McGee singing...

LINDA   "My Daddy, His Gibson Guitar and Me".

HOSS   Whoopee!!!

LINDA starts to play and sing. STAN and DANIELLE fill in harmonies and for the first time STAN, on guitar, is up front too.

MY DADDY, HIS GIBSON GUITAR AND ME

LINDA   First thing I remember
Well my Daddy sang to me
Playing Wildwood Flower
With his guitar on his knee.
Honky tonks and truck stops
We were wild and free
Eatin' up the blacktop
My Daddy, his Gibson guitar and me.

ALL   It was just a flat top box
The frets are all wore down
Not too much to look at
But I still can hear the sound
Of my Daddy singing
Sweet mountain harmony

LINDA   My Daddy, his Gibson guitar and me.
But a picture comes some nights
A broken tavern door
Lyin' in the back seat
Of my daddy's beat up Ford.

LINDA Inside well they were playing
"Movin' On", then ""Jambalaya""
I was huggin on my mandolin
And trying not to cry.

ALL It was just a flat top box
The frets are all wore down
Wasn't much to look at
But I still can hear the sound
Of my Daddy singing
Sweet mountain harmony

LINDA My Daddy, his Gibson guitar and me.

Don't you worry Daddy, I'll be all right
Don't you worry Daddy, you taught me right

ALL We'll reach into the night
And pull us down a star

LINDA Just me and my Daddy's Gibson guitar

The day my Daddy passed on
He left me this old guitar
Said I ain't got nothin' else
And it won't take you too far
But this guitar is full of dreams
And dreams can set you free
Now I dream about the old times
My Daddy, his Gibson guitar and me.

ALL Well it's just a flat top box
The frets are all wore down
Not too much to look at
But I still can hear the sound
Of my Daddy singing
Sweet mountain harmony

LINDA My Daddy, his Gibson guitar and me.

ALL Well it's just a flat top box
The frets are all wore down
Not too much to look at
But I still can hear the sound
Of my Daddy singing
Sweet mountain harmony

LINDA My Daddy, his Gibson guitar and me.
My Daddy, his Gibson guitar and me

HOSS Cut! And print it.

DANIELLE   (*to LINDA*) Honey, that was beautiful. We're in. (*to STAN*) Stanley, you're coming home with me. Now.

STAN   Yes!

> *STAN hurries off to get his stuff.*

DANIELLE   Meet me out front, hon. (*to LINDA*) I'm in love.

> *DANIELLE exits with the video camera, singing.*

It was just a flat top box
The frets are all wore down
Not too much to look at...

HOSS   Some good song, Linda. And...and that's the first one you finished that's a real story about yourself, isn't it?

LINDA   Yeah.

HOSS   Ah...sorry about tellin' on you not reading.

LINDA   That's OK, Hoss. Now that everybody knows the truth I don't have to hide anymore.

HOSS   Yeah, you just speak the truth and believe in what's right and everything works out — most times.

LINDA   (*pause*) Listen Hoss, about what happened the other night...

HOSS   That's OK, Linda. I know. Just...easier if you don't say, eh? Do something for me though?

LINDA   Sure Hoss. What?

HOSS   Promise to win the contest on Bobby.

LINDA   I promise.

> *LINDA takes his hand and squeezes. HOSS beams. Blackout.*

Act Two, Scene Five

"Bobby's Bump" is heard in the black.

BOBBY (*Voice Over*) And we'll be back real soon with the final two contestants in the Cross Canada Country Countdown, "Linda McGee" and "The Fabulous Kelly Conners"!

The band buttons the tag as the lights come up on HOSS and LINDA in the dressing room. They're playing Fish.

HOSS Got any Jacks?

LINDA Fish. Got any Aces?

HOSS checks his hand.

HOSS Fish.

STAN walks in and HOSS deals him a hand. STAN is wearing a red Nudie suit.

STAN You guys are up next.

LINDA I'm terrified.

HOSS You're gonna win. You promised. Got any fives?

STAN   Fish.

                *HOSS draws. DANIELLE enters, flamboyant as
                ever.*

DANIELLE   My God, they are lined up down to Mr. Transmission
                and the place is already full!

LINDA   Wish you were singing lead on this thing.

DANIELLE   Linda, I am not a great country singer. You are.

LINDA   You sing fine.

DANIELLE   True, but I'm really a samba kind of gal, right
                Stanley?

STAN   Just like Astrid Gilberta.

                *DANIELLE gives STANLEY a kiss and sits
                beside him on his chair.*

LINDA   Samba's?

DANIELLE   Si. They're Brazilian! (*sings to STAN*) "Tall and tan
                and young and handsome".

LINDA   Oh, I know all about sambas. Tex used to do "Yellow
                Bird".

STAN   Ouch.

DANIELLE   Linda? I'm sorry for what I said about Tex.

LINDA   No. It was true. (*pause*) He just spent too many years
                in the bars and it broke his heart. But he really loved
                me, Danielle. He gave me everything he had to give.
                Guess it wasn't much.

HOSS   (*joking, but serious too*) He gave you lots; the
                  wonderful gift of music and a heart that's true.

                  LINDA and DANIELLE laugh. He beams.

DANIELLE   I'm sorry I screwed up, Linda.

LINDA   You told me! You told me!

DANIELLE   I meant it! I meant it!

HOSS   Got any eights?

DANIELLE   Nope.

STAN   She means...

STAN &
DANIELLE   Fish.

DANIELLE   Got any kings?

                  *LINDA sighs dramatically and hands her three
                  kings. DANIELLE puts down a set and laughs.*

DANIELLE   Jacks?

HOSS
& LINDA   Fish.

                  KELLY enters, strutting to hide her discomfort.

KELLY   How's it goin' kids?

LINDA   (*ignoring her*) Got any queens, Hoss?

HOSS   Just you. Go Fish. Got any threes?

KELLY	Look, I know how you feel and I can't blame you, but that doesn't change anything. You do your best, because I'm going to give it everything I got.
DANIELLE	Yikes!

DANIELLE hands HOSS a three.

KELLY	None of this would have happened if it wasn't for you, Danielle.
DANIELLE	It wouldn't have happened if you hadn't chosen to cohabitate with swamp slime, right Stanley?
STAN	I pass.
KELLY	Neither of us has any room to criticize Bobby. I'm a jealous jerk and you're a....
DANIELLE	Yes, speak?
KELLY	(*controlling her temper*) All I'm saying is that as far as Daddy's Girl's goes Bobby played it by the book and he played it right. If Linda hadn't been so pig-headed...
LINDA	She wouldn't be standing on her own two legs for the first time.
KELLY	He did the best he could.
DANIELLE	He's a rat who'd sell your first born for a hit.
KELLY	Amanda doesn't need a hit record and I've already had one. What we both need is him. I'm not raising my kid alone. I'm not going back to The Can Car Plant and if you think I'm gonna spend the rest of my life sleeping in an empty bed, you are out of your mind.
DANIELLE	(*sings*) "Looking for love in all the wrong places..."

KELLY   Danielle, he fired you because *I told him to*. He did it
        for me and if...ah, what's the use? None of you hear a
        word I'm saying.

        Silence. A long tense moment.

HOSS   You know how to play Fish?

KELLY   Hoss, everybody plays Fish.

HOSS   Want to sit in?

KELLY   What?

HOSS   Fish! You want to play fish?

KELLY   No.

        HOSS winks at KELLY. What's he up to?

KELLY   I mean...you really want me to play?

HOSS   'Fraid Danielle'll beat you?

KELLY   Deal me in.

        HOSS does.

HOSS   Got any Jacks?

KELLY   Go fish. (*to DANIELLE*) Got any twos?

        *DANIELLE hands KELLY twos, she lays her
        cards down.*

KELLY   Sixes?

        DANIELLE reaches for her hand.

HOSS   You got to say "Got any"

KELLY   OK. Got any sixes?

HOSS   Too late. Miss a turn.

                   HOSS winks at DANIELLE. BOBBY enters.

BOBBY   Five minutes.

LINDA   Oh God.

                   *LINDA throws down her hand and goes to the
                   make up table. She starts to fuss with her hair.
                   HOSS picks up her hand. STAN stands,
                   grabbing a bottle of mineral water.*

STAN   Better check my charts.

DANIELLE   That's my Stan...

STAN   ...the Evian man.

                   *DANIELLE laughs. STAN waves the bottle at
                   her and exits.*

HOSS   Switch directions. Danielle. Got any tens?

DANIELLE   Fish. (*to KELLY*) Got any sixes?

                   *KELLY gives her two sixes. DANIELLE lays
                   down.*

BOBBY   Listen Linda, I just want to say, no hard feelings.
                   Remember, if "Friends" is a hit you're going to make
                   a bundle.

DANIELLE   Eights?

KELLY   Miss a turn.

HOSS   You got to say; "Got any".

BOBBY   (*exasperated*) I just don't get it. Why screw that up?
             You go out there, sing your little ditty, and you'll
             split the vote right down the middle. Bingo! We all
             lose.

DANIELLE   Wrong. Linda is going to win.

BOBBY   Sorry, but with Kelly singing "Friends" I don't like
             the odds.

KELLY   Bobby, chill out.

BOBBY   I'm just trying to talk sense.

HOSS   Cool it, Bobby.

BOBBY   I'm not talking to you, Hoss.

HOSS   (*stands*) That's right. I'm talking to you. Linda's
             singing no matter what you say and she's gonna win
             so...go piss up a tree.

             They all laugh. Slowly BOBBY begins to smile.

BOBBY   Right.

             *BOBBY offers HOSS his hand. HOSS shakes it.
             BOBBY starts to exit.*

KELLY   Bobby?

BOBBY   Yeah, babe?

KELLY   You play good for her.

BOBBY   Damn it, Kelly, we're on national TV. I am going to
             play great for her.

             BOBBY exits.

HOSS   Got any nines?

> *DANIELLE hands him nines. KELLY takes a
> deep breath.*

KELLY   So...I heard your run-through. Good song, but don't
drag the tempo. It's an anthem, not a dirge.

> *LINDA's hair is a mess and she can't seem to get
> it right.*

LINDA   Anthem, dirge, I'm gonna lose and we both know it.

HOSS   Bobby wouldn't have said all that stuff if he wasn't
scared you were going to win. Right, Kelly?

KELLY   Well, you're definitely more threat than an Elvis
impersonator.

> *DANIELLE laughs. She and KELLY smile at
> each other for just a second.*

KELLY   Danielle, look at her hair.

> *KELLY gestures at LINDA's disarrayed hair.*

KELLY   That rat's nest could be concealing a truck! Fix it.

DANIELLE   You just sealed your fate, dear.

> *DANIELLE throws down her hand and grabs a
> brush. She goes to work. HOSS picks up her
> hand.*

KELLY   I don't want to win because Linda's having a bad hair
day!

HOSS   Got any kings?

> *KELLY hands him kings. LINDA won't sit still.*

DANIELLE   Linda, sit still!

HOSS   Jacks?

LINDA   I can't. I can't do it.

KELLY   Here take them all!

> *KELLY hands HOSS all her cards and crosses to LINDA. HOSS sorts his hand rapidly.*

KELLY   Linda, now you stop. Listen to me. If you want to win...

LINDA   I can't win. You're the best!

HOSS   You can do anything you want, if you don't cheat yourself by givin' up.

> *Inspecting the huge hand carefully, HOSS breaks into a grin.*

HOSS   See, you can't win nothing unless you try. You make a wish and then you Fish.

> *HOSS lays everything down! They all laugh. In the bar LINDA's music begins to play. LINDA puts out her hands. DANIELLE and KELLY take them.*

KELLY   Ahhh.

DANIELLE   Ahhh.

LINDA   Ahhh.

ALL   Ah!!!!

> *They exit the dressing room. On stage BOBBY goes into his intro.*

BOBBY   Ladies and Gentlemen, the first time I heard one of
this little lady's songs I knew she was something
special. Well, she's come a long way since then and
I'm sure she's just going to get better and better so
please give a warm round of applause to Linda
McGee.

*The band kicks in. LINDA and DANIELLE come
on. LINDA looks at the crowd, nervously and
then motions to the band to play softer.*

LINDA   Thank you. Ah...this is a song called "Heroes" and it
wasn't the song got me into this contest. See, I just
wrote it and well, I think it's important that what it's
got to say gets said tonight. It's about somebody who
tried to teach me to be brave, and I guess it's
working, 'cause here I am. And this contest? Well it
doesn't really matter if I win or lose, 'cause just
standing up here means I already won. So this is for
Jerry Cartright, who taught me to be brave.

*LINDA looks at HOSS who stands at the far end
of the bar watching. He beams. She sings
"Heroes"to him.*

HEROES

LINDA   My heroes have always been singers of songs
Who stand tall with their backs to the wall
Who swallow their heartbreak and endure the pain
That can come like a curse to us all

The fighters and writers, the women of strength
Who some how and some way survive
With a family and no man, on welfare who can
Still stand proud and say still I'm alive

And I guess I need heroes
People whose spirits are strong
And I guess I need heroes

To bend and not break
Heroes who stand in for us all

Now I have a friend, and you know he's a man
Who got dealt a bum hand still he sings
He got deuces, no Aces some threes and a five
But his heart well it makes him a king.

And he is a hero
A man whose spirit is strong
Yeah he is a hero
Who no matter what, somehow goes on
He's gentle, he's wise
He's a man who won't lie
He sees the hero inside of us all.

He says;
"You don't need to fuss
You don't need to fight
You just speak the truth
And believe in what's right"
He says; "It's everyday folks
Make the difference in life."
Take us out of the darkness
And into the light

We all need to be heroes
People who spirits are strong
Yeah we all need to be heroes
Who no matter what somehow go on
Be gentle and wise
Don't fall for no lies
'Cause there's a hero inside of us all.

Be gentle and wise
Don't fall for no lies
'Cause there's a hero inside of us all.
There's a hero inside of us all.

> *Song ends. LINDA steps forward and bows.*
> *Applause. Blackout.*

Act Two, Scene Six

Lights up on HOSS who is standing at the pay phone reading a letter. He dials a number and pumps quarters into the machine. As the phone rings he reads the letter again. LINDA appears in a special on the far side of the stage.

LINDA   Dear Hoss; This is the first letter I have ever written by myself all alone. I never even shown it to Betty, who is my tutor, at Literacy. I just wanted to write and say I miss you and to send you the words to my newest song which is kinda about what happened to us, but...well you know how stories get changed when you have to make them rhyme. Anyway hope you like it. Guess which heart you are?

HOSS is practically bouncing up and down in anticipation as the phone is answered.

HOSS   Hi...Linda.? Hi! It's Hoss. Yeah, I got your letter and ...you're writing good! Yeah, some good school, eh? I tip my Stetson hat to that. (*pause*) So, long time no see, huh? Yeah, and pats on the back. Gettin on *Rita McNeil and Friends*. Yeah. That's somethin'. Yeah! And, and you know what? Danielle and Stan got a new band. Yeah; "Brazil 747" They play "The Airliner" on weekends.

HOSS   Me? I'm great. I'm workin' at the TV Station now!
It's OK, but they don't let me read the news!
(*laughing*). Hey...hey, you know where I am right
now? Give you a hint — it's Talent Night. (*pause*)
Yeah, sure, I come down all the time. You know
Bobby — he can't hold a grudge and now that Kelly's
gonna get another baby...Yeah! And Bobby keeps on
backing his car into things all the time!

So, now that you're a star and all, you gonna come
here on tour or something? (*pause*) No, it's just
'cause I think about it sometimes. You know you
come in, and everybody is here to meet you and
Bobby? You know Bobby, he gets up and says he
"discovered you", which is true, so when he asks you
to come up and sing a song with Kelly and Danielle
well you'd do it. And, wow, Daddy's Girls are up
there on stage! And then he's gonna say "Hoss, get
your happy ass up here," and we're all together again.
Like in a dream — when everything comes true.

Ah.. Hello? Operator? No I'm out of quarters...Linda?
I got to go. No quarters, but I got to (*sings*)
"Tell you I love you, I swear every night"
Hello? Linda? (*he's been disconnected*) It's true. I love
you Linda. Goodnight.

HOSS hangs up and looks at LINDA's letter.
Lights shifts, music begins. We enter a dream.

BOBBY   Hoss, get your happy ass down here. We got a song
for you.

DANIELLE, KELLY and LINDA appear dressed
as Daddy's Girls and glide towards the mikes.
The band plays the intro to "Cheatin' Hearts".

CHEATIN' HEARTS

THE GIRLS Well there are hearts of gold
Hearts full of soul
Hearts on Fire
Filled with desire
Restless hearts
Ain't never satisfied
A heart like yours
Or a heart like mine

You know a true heart
Can be a blue heart
Hearts can grow cold
Then hearts can be sold
Everybody's heart
Gets broken some time
A heart like yours
Or a heart like mine.

So you better watch out
For the cheatin' heart
She's the Queen of Spades
In the game of love
You'd better beware
She's called the black lady
And the deck is stacked
Against the cheatin' heart

The cast start trading off lines.

THE GIRLS So listen to me
In the game of love
Cheaters never win
They scramble to the top
Then tumble down again
The heart can be a joker
The heart can turn to stone
And if your heart keeps cheatin'
You'll end — end up all alone

BOBBY And every beatin' heart
Can be a cheatin' heart
So you better leave
That extra ace up your sleeve

B. & K Or you're going to find
Your hearts the achin' kind

ALL A heart like yours
Or a heart like mine

LINDA   Give it a shot
Play the hand that you've got
If you don't cheat

ALL   Then you can never get caught

So you better watch out
For the cheatin' heart
She's the Queen of Spades
In the game of love
You'd better beware
She's called the black lady
And the deck is stacked
Against the cheatin', cheatin', heart

Watch out for the cheatin' heart
You better watch out
Watch out for the cheatin' heart
You better watch out
Watch out for the cheatin' heart
You better watch out
Watch out for the cheatin' heart
Watch out, watch out, watch out
For the cheatin' heart.

*The song ends. The three women look at each
other for a long moment and then hug and laugh.
LINDA reaches out and takes HOSS' hand,
bringing him up on stage. KELLY hugs
BOBBY. For one brief magic they are all there
together. They take their bow. Curtain.*

The End.

Selected Songs

THERE AIN'T NOTHIN' LIKE A FRIEND

YOU'VE GOT TO HAVE A GIMMICK

HEROES